# CLASSIC SPORTS AND SUPERCARS

Published in 1995 by
Regency House Publishing Limited
The Grange, Grange Yard
London SE1 3AG

ISBN 1 85361 410 6

Printed in China

*Front Cover*
Chrysler's Viper RT/10

Back cover
1994 Aston Martin Virage Litre Conversion

*Page 2 and 3*
1993 McLaren F1, No XP-5 pre-production
prototype

*Right*
1959 Chevrolet Corvette

Picture acknowledgements

All photographs are © Neill Bruce, except the
Corvette ZR1, which is courtesy of Chevrolet press
office. I would like to thank all the press offices
and generous owners who have patiently allowed
their cars to be photographed. Particular thanks
are extended to Nigel and Michael Dawes, who
between them provided the Alfa Romeo, Allard,
Bentley S1, 1954 Corvette, Invicta, Jaguar XK150 S
Coupé, Jaguar V12 E-type roadster and the Porsche
911 Carrera RS. The excellent Midland Motor
Museum, in Bridgnorth, UK provided the BMW
3.00 CSL, Bugatti T 57, DeLorean, Ford GT40,
Frazer Nash, and both Mercedes-Benz 300SLs.
Philip Jones, of Byron Garages International
organized the unique blue Aston Martin DB4 GT
Zagato. Brooks Auctioneers provided the
Willment Cobra, The Jaguar E-type 2+2, and the
Vauxhall. Many thanks to the development
engineers of McLaren Cars Ltd., who parked the F1
so neatly in between test laps of a secret circuit,
and let me grab some shots of the most stunning
car I've ever experienced. Also Peter Lovett of
Dick Lovett Sportscars, who nearly froze to death
whilst I shot the Porsche 959 one chilly November
afternoon. Finally, I cannot omit my dear friend
Roger Stowers, Aston Martin Lagonda's Historian
and Archivist, who has so ably looked after visiting
photographers for many years. A day at Aston
Martin is a day to look forward to, especially with
Roger driving me in the latest model to some quiet
spot where I can work in peace.

Neill Bruce.
Burghclere, England 1995

# CLASSIC SPORTS AND SUPERCARS

## Doug Nye

### With Neill Bruce

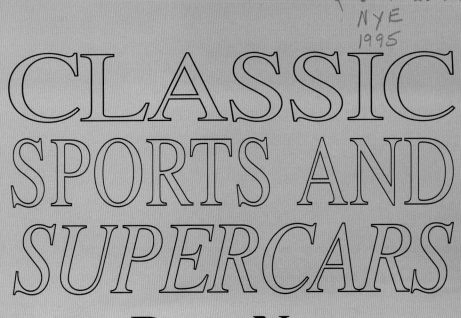

Regency House Publishing Ltd.

# FOREWORD

Way back in the 1950s, endless discussion filled the columns of the specialist motoring press in response to the question 'What is a sports car?' A suitably precise definition proved elusive, and the most sensible answer that I recall was along the lines of 'We cannot specify precisely what a sports car may be, but we can assure you that you'll know it when you see one...'

Through the 1960s, what had previously been pure sports car performance became available in an ever widening range of saloon touring cars, starting perhaps with the Mini-Cooper and Lotus Cortina and then extending notably through the various roofed-in sporting products of Alfa Romeo, BMW, Ford and other similar leading manufacturers.

In the 1970s the term 'Supercar' came to be applied to the handful of true exotics which began to appear, cars which were manufactured most notably by Lamborghini, Ferrari, Maserati and Porsche. These tended to be cars which were intended more for extremely high performance upon the public road than upon the race circuits of the world. As such there was little way of comparing their relative capabilities beyond academic comparison with the stopwatch along an acceleration strip or maximum speed test-straight.

For any of us who had been brought up in motor racing this was a rather unsatisfactory state of affairs, with all this airy talk of 0-60mph in under 6 seconds and 170mph-plus top speeds translating merely to a traffic lights Grand Prix and the depressing spectacle of the over-rich posing in some truly preposterous and impracticable motor cars around Monte Carlo's Casino Square. This was, however, to apply a cynical outlook to the best that the production car industry could offer, and the real point was that many of the so-called Supercars were good enough to deserve better owners who were more enthusiastic and proficient than most – in short, those owners who had their hearts in the right place.

What follows in these pages takes a look at a cross-section of some of the world's greatest sports and Supercars through the lens of Neill Bruce's camera – recording the good, the bad, the brilliant and in some instances the just plain ugly. But all these cars have one thing in common – within the context of their time they were all capable of what could be described as high performance; they were among the very fastest and finest cars around, the best available sports and Supercars of their day.

*Doug Nye*

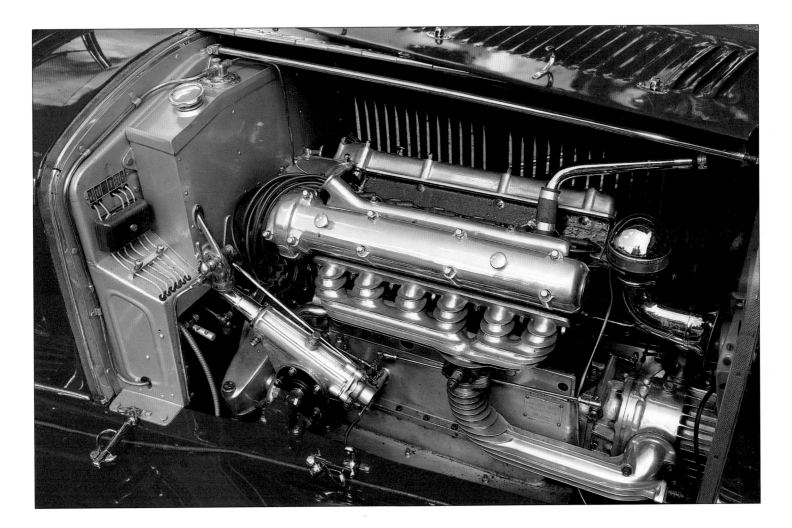

# ALFA ROMEO 1750

The Alfa Romeo 1750 was undoubtedly one of the greatest products of the world-famous Milanese marque during the Vintage period between the two World Wars.

With the introduction of its 6-cylinder 1500 model, Alfa Romeo had initially armed itself with a new category of cars which were defined as Gran Turismo designs – offering genuine long-distance touring potential but allied to new standards of high performance.

For many Alfa Romeo customers, the 6C-1500 was the answer to their prayers with the only limitation being its confined 1500cc power potential, particularly in the more mountainous areas of the home market.

Consequently, the enlarged

*The great strength of the 6C-1750 was its exquisitely crafted 6-cylinder engine, one of the first high-performance production power units to prove itself truly reliable at sustained high rpm on high speed Roman roads.*

---

**ALFA ROMEO 1750**
**1930**

**Top speed:** 95 mph

**Engine:** In-line 6-cylinder supercharged

**Bore x Stroke:** 65mm x 88mm

**Capacity:** 1752cc

**Wheelbase:** 9ft 0ins (2743mm)

**Track:** 4ft 6ins (front)/4ft 6ins (rear) - 1371mm/1371mm

---

6C-1750 was developed to run even more smoothly, to produce considerably improved torque and to make the most of a lithe and limber chassis which guaranteed the best road-holding available by the standards of the time.

The single-overhead camshaft Turismo model was launched in the *Salone dell'Automobile* in Rome in January, 1929, and in April 1930 a twin-overhead camshaft Super Sport variant stood all Italy on its ear by winning the greatest motor sporting event of the period – the 1,000 mile Mille Miglia road race.

This victory by Giuseppe Campari/Giulio Ramponi was a tremendous publicity coup for Alfa Romeo, and upon its shirt tails the always expensive 1750s became a commercial success far exceeding that of the preceding 1500.

Two particular variants were widely used in competition, the

*Super Sport* (SS) and *Gran Sport* (GS) amongst a complex series of production variants, some fitted with light-alloy cylinder heads, others with monobloc engines in cast iron and all with differing performance potential. The 1750's sporting career extended far beyond production which ceased in 1933, the many open road races of the period becoming its natural habitat.

Production of the 1750 SS and GS totalled only 269 units of all series while two sextets of racing 6C-1750SS

and GS cars were made – one in 1929, the other in 1930 – and 159 supercharged models emerged in 1931-32. The end of the line came in the 6th Series *Gran Sport* of 1933 – with stiffened chassis – which ran to 44 units.

Behind the wheel of a 1750 one is immediately impressed by its well-weighted and direct steering, nimble handling and reassuringly powerful drum brakes. The cars simply feel well-balanced, nimble and rapid, with

a nicely responsive and smooth 6-cylinder engine, offering muscular torque in its supercharged forms. Lovely cars, by any standard.

*Carrozzeria Zagato's rakishly aggressive body styling for the Alfa Romeo 6C-1750 has helped make this model one of the most sought-after of all the great classic vintage sports cars. This example, chassis 6C-8513042, had been restored by British connoisseur, Nigel Dawes.*

# ALLARD J2X

Sydney Allard was a great British motor sporting character of the years around the Second World War, and his Allard Motor Company of Clapham, South London, really made its name with the American V8-engined J2 model which was introduced at the London Motor Show of 1949.

In those dark days of postwar recession, in a nation effectively bankrupted by six years of fighting democracy's war, the huge majority of British motor industry production was channelled into overseas export markets. Any new car was at a premium, and second-hand car prices were astronomic. Consequently, many enthusiasts beat a trail to Allard's door as a source of brand-new sporting cars, but in truth the product was rather agricultural and primitive in the extreme.

The J2 featured minimalist bodywork, was light, stark and strong, and for the British market it was powered by 3.9-litre overhead valve Mercury-Ardun V8s. For cars sold in the lucrative U.S. market larger 'lumps' were adopted, including the 5.4-litre Cadillac and Chrysler V8s and the impressive Oldsmobile Rocket.

The J2X carried its engine some $7^1/_2$ inches further forward and had a 6-inch longer nose overhang than the original J2 – 'X' for 'Xtra'!

Syd Allard then won the 1952 Monte Carlo Rally outright with his P-Type saloon to earn real respectability for his marque, but by that time Jaguar's XK120 was cornering the specialist large-capacity sports car market. Since the choice then lay between a major manufacturer's value-for-money full production model – backed-up by proper dealer network support virtually worldwide – and a virtual one-off car handbuilt in a tiny and primitive factory in Clapham, South London, Allard's market died and after 1958 the company concentrated upon producing tuning

*Every spartan inch of the Allard J2X breathed sheer, uncompromising brutal power – and the big American Cadillac V8 beneath that light-weight aluminium hood provided it. No one could describe the Allard J2 series as beautiful sports cars, but they have immense period charm.*

parts for a range of Ford saloons.

Yet despite all the above, for an elbows-out, flies in the teeth, muscular hurtle around winding country roads, with the evocative throb of a big slow-revving V8 on tap beneath the driver's right foot – the primitive charms of the Allard J2X remain undeniably attractive.

## ALLARD J2X
### 1952

**Top speed:** 125 mph

**Engine:** 90-degree V8

**Bore x Stroke:** 84.1mm x 98.4mm

**Capacity:** 4375cc

**Wheelbase:** 8ft 4ins (2540mm)

**Track:** 4ft 8ins (front)/4ft 8ins (rear) - 1422mm/1422mm

# AMC JAVELIN

The American Motors Corporation
was founded as recently as 1954 by the
merger of Nash and Hudson. Even
then, the two marques' individual
products continued to be marketed
under their original names until 1958
when the corporate title of 'Rambler'
was adopted. Subsequently, it was the
Javelin model which became the first
AMC product to use the initials for its
own marque title as in 1968 the
ineffective and little-regarded Rambler
tag was quietly dropped.

AMC's objective with the Javelin
had been to blaze a commercial trail
into the sport coupé market which was
then proving so attractive and
commercially successful within what
had become very much the young
man's motoring market, dominated at
the time by Ford's Mustang and
Chevrolet's Camaro.

The shapely if rather fussily-styled
new Javelin was offered with a choice
of 4.8-, 5.6- and 6.4-litre V8 engines,
while a less expensive alternative was
available in a 3.8-litre in-line 'six'. The
Javelin was also supported by the
shorter-wheelbase AMX Coupé which
used the same range of V8 engines,
but this smaller vehicle was
withdrawn after 1971.

Meanwhile, for the 1972 sales year,
AMC's marketeers tried to corner
some really top-market cachet for the
Javelin by introducing their
re-specified 'Cardin' model which
boasted – or some would say suffered
from – an interior designed by the
Parisian haute couturier Pierre Cardin.

The top model Javelin was
undoubtedly an impressive device,
with its big 6.4-litre V8 developing
325bhp at a lazy 5,000rpm, but it was a
heavy car and its somewhat quirky
styling had not endowed it with the
most aerodynamically penetrative of
body shapes. In part consequence its
0-60mph acceleration time was not as
impressive as one might have
expected, at 7.6secs, and its top speed
in standard form was only 120mph.

*An unpromoted and relatively under-stated
American candidate for the sports, if not quite
Supercar, tag, the American Motors
Corporation's shapely Javelin packed
considerable punch.*

Yet AMC Javelins were modified and
race tuned for American TransAm
Championship saloon car competition
and with Roger Penske's legendary
team direction and preparation and
Mark Donohue's driving they humb-
led Ford and Chevrolet. This TransAm
Championship success was a mighty
feather in AMC's cap, but they could
only dent Ford and General Motors'
pride, never topple it.

---

## AMC JAVELIN 390
### 1970

**Top speed:** 120 mph

**Engine:** 90-degree V8

**Bore x Stroke:** 105.9mm x 90.7mm

**Capacity:** 6391cc

**Wheelbase:** 9ft 2ins (2791mm)

**Track:** 4ft 11ins (front)/4ft 8$\frac{1}{2}$ ins
(rear) - 1501mm/1438mm

## ASTON MARTIN DB2

*The subject of an extensive restoration of exquisite high-quality, this 1950 Aston Martin DB2, chassis serial LML/50/179, has been claimed to be the World's best. The restoration work itself is reputed to have cost more than £90,000!*

When millionaire industrialist David Brown bought the failing Aston Martin and Lagonda companies in 1947, he was indulging his enormous personal enthusiasm for high-performance bespoke cars. His ownership of course, was the reason why Aston Martin models adopted their 'DB' type-number initials, and although the tag was never really used, the replacement DB2 model made its public debut in 1949 in the most dramatic manner as a works team of three of the cars contested the revived Le Mans 24-Hours marathon race.

Two of these works-team DB2 aerodynamic coupés were equipped with the DB1's 2-litre 4-cylinder engine, while the third employed a new 2.6-litre twin-overhead camshaft 6-cylinder unit created by none other than the veteran design engineer W.O. Bentley, of pre-war Bentley Motors fame, for the postwar Lagonda. In 1950 this fine unit combined with the handsome coupé body in the production DB2. Relatively hefty to handle, but undeniably quick, comfortable and glamorous, the DB2 launched the modern Aston Martin breed.

# ASTON MARTIN DB2
## 1952

**Top speed:** 125 mph

**Engine:** In-line twin-overhead camshaft 6-cylinder

**Bore x Stroke:** 78mm x 90mm

**Capacity:** 2580cc

**Wheelbase:** 8ft 3ins (2514mm)

**Track:** 4ft 6ins (front)/4ft 6ins (rear) - 1371mm/1371mm

**RIGHT**

*The six-cylinder twin-cam engine of the Aston Martin DB2 was derived from a W.O. Bentley design for the Lagonda marque which had been acquired together with Aston Martin by British industrialist David Brown – hence the 'DB' prefix for the cars.*

**BELOW**

*The driver sits deep within the DB2 cockpit, conscious of the high scuttle and coachwork waistline around him. Although the controls are heavy and fatiguing by modern standards, the DB2 was a delight to drive in its day.*

# ASTON MARTIN DB4 GT ZAGATO

## ASTON MARTIN DB4 GT ZAGATO
### 1962

**Top speed:** 165 mph

**Engine:** 6-cylinder In-line

**Bore x Stroke:** 92mm x 92mm

**Capacity:** 3670cc

**Wheelbase:** 7ft 9ins (2362mm)

**Track:** 4ft 6½ ins (front)/4ft 5ins (rear) - 1384mm/1346mm

In 1959, Aston Martin won both the Le Mans 24-Hours classic race and the Sports Car World Championship with its DBR1/300 open-cockpit sports-racing cars. Owner David Brown was happy for the company to rest upon its laurels, where the marque was concerned, after this double-headed success; during 1960 – 61 motor racing regulations evolved to replace open

sports car competition with a series of endurance races aimed more at closed-top *Gran Turismo* designs.

These cars were intended to be more in keeping with those which would be available to the public, and Aston Martin responded with a select batch of 19 short-wheelbase, lightweight-bodied versions of their already scarce but successful DB4GT model, with coachwork designed and built by the Carrozzeria Zagato company of Milan, Italy.

The DB4GT model itself had been introduced at the 1959 London Motor Show, and it was already Italian-bodied in light-weight aluminium form, by Carrozzeria Touring in their *Superleggera* (super lightweight) style. Its 3.7-litre twin-overhead camshaft 6-

cylinder engine produced a thumping 302bph at 6,000rpm, and a year later the Zagato version, Aston Martin's even more charismatic and muscular sister model, was launched with its engine's power output raised to a minimum 314bhp.

Two of these DB4GT Zagatos in particular became famous, the pair registered '1 VEV' and '2 VEV' which were deployed by John Ogier's private Essex Racing Stable team. These two cars shone brightly in competition in the hands of such racing personalities as Jim Clark, Roy Salvadori, Innes Ireland, Tony Maggs and Sir John Whitmore. But here we are more concerned with the road-going versions which comprised the majority of Newport Pagnell-cum-Milanese production, and which basked in reflected glory from the two 'VEVs'.

Today, all the surviving DB4GT Zagatos are highly prized as perhaps the most special of quantity production *Gran Turismo* Aston Martins.

**ABOVE**
*Only 19 of the gloriously brutish aluminium-bodied DB4GT Zagatos were produced, all but one with the faired-in competition-type headlight design seen here.*

**LEFT**
*Exception to the rule: this Aston Martin DB4 GT Zagato, chassis serial 0188, is the only one to be produced with unfaired external-mounted headlights rather resembling a Ferrari 250GT Short Wheel-Base.*

# ASTON MARTIN VANTAGE

In October 1993, Aston Martin Lagonda, by that time the most aristocratic satellite of the mighty Ford Motor Company, announced a stunningly specified 550 horse power Aston Martin Vantage. For years, Aston had supplied this name to the most highly-tuned variants of standard models within its range. Now the Vantage with all its connotations of performance 'Ad-Vantage' took unprecedented strides.

While the standard 5.3-litre four-cam V8 Aston saloon was more than adequate for the majority of customers, there remained many enthusiasts demanding an even higher level of performance. For them the Newport Pagnell factory now applied twin Eaton superchargers with water inter-cooling (to keep incoming fuel/air charge, as compressed by the superchargers, cool and dense despite its pressurization), and with Ford EEC IV electronic 'computerized' engine management. A fully catalytic exhaust system was applied and the Vantage even ran on environmentally-friendly leadfree fuel.

Vivid performance was guaranteed by its twin supercharged engine's peak power of 550bhp at 6,500rpm twinned with maximum torque at 4,000rpm. Driving through a six-speed gearbox, the Vantage could punch its way from 0-60mph in a lung-crushing 4.6 seconds and on to 100mph in 10.1, despite the basic car's considerable – many would still say gross – size and weight. For so much 'Go' there had to be extra 'Stop', which was provided by the largest ventilated disc brakes ever fitted to a production car, their callipers being taken directly from the shelved Aston Martin Group C 'Le Mans' racing coupé.

Not for nothing did Aston Martin invite all Vantage owners to join an advanced driving programme at the Goodwood circuit, conducted by former McLaren and BRM F1 driver

Peter Gethin, before taking delivery of their new car!

The Vantage body was hand-crafted, of course, in aluminium, upon a robust steel chassis complete with side-intrusion barriers within the doors and airbag protection for both driver and front-seat passenger. The big V8 modern Aston Martins are very much an acquired taste, but the combination of Olde Worlde craftsmanship and tangible quality, together with modern Ford high technology standards created something uniquely attractive and in keeping with the traditional old Aston Martin theme. Certainly the prodigious adrenalin-pumping performance of such a palpably large car compensated for its antiquated

standard of specific design, packaging, and innovation. But then they never were intended to appeal to lovers of the Lotus Elan.

---

### ASTON MARTIN VANTAGE
#### 1993

**Top speed:** 186 mph

**Engine:** 90-degree four-cam V8

**Bore x Stroke:** 100mm x 85mm

**Capacity:** 5340cc

**Wheelbase:** 8ft 6ins (2590mm)

**Track:** 5ft 1ins (front)/5ft 2$\frac{1}{2}$ins (rear) – 1548mm/1586mm

---

**ABOVE**
*Imposing power house for the Aston Martin Vantage – the 4-camshaft V8 engines are individually assembled in the finest tradition, for many years even bearing the engine builder's name.*

**LEFT**
*Stunning hand-built craftsmanship and sheer, mind-boggling performance potential – the Aston Martin Vantage breathes bulldog spirit.*

# BENTLEY SPEED SIX BLUE TRAIN COUPÉ

During the 1930s France's *Train Bleu* express, the 'Blue Train', was second only in fame to the Orient Express. It ran from Cannes on the Mediterranean Côte d'Azur to Paris and, at a time when only the wealthy could afford a vacation on the exotic French Riviera the idea of a race against the Blue Train had a special cachet.

Bentley Motors Ltd was backed by one of its finest and most enthusiastic amateur racing drivers, the multi-millionaire Woolf 'Babe' Barnato. His family fortune had been made in the South African diamond strikes at Kimberley, and in 1916 Woolf had inherited a cool half-million pounds from his father and uncle. He was a natural sportsman. At Cambridge University he had proved himself a ferocious boxer, a fine shot, an expert horseman, and a brilliant skier. He played county cricket for Surrey and was a two-handicap golfer. And then came his motor racing...

He had quickly latched onto W.O. Bentley's big, fast and reliable sports cars and from May 1926 Woolf Barnato became Bentley Motors' major backer. But as a driver he always took W.O.'s orders, and he was brilliant at nursing a car, reliably and quickly, to the finish of the most demanding endurance races.

At various times Barnato actually owned at least three 3-litre Bentleys, three 4$\frac{1}{2}$s, two Blower 4$\frac{1}{2}$s, no fewer than six 6$\frac{1}{2}$s, three Speed Sixes and five of the ultimate 8-litre models.

Shortly after winning the Le Mans 24-Hours race in 1929, sharing a 6$\frac{1}{2}$-litre with his friend Sir Henry 'Tim' Birkin, Barnato had ordered a similar 6$\frac{1}{2}$ of his own with a closed saloon body.

He chose the 140$\frac{1}{2}$-inch wheelbase option from the four available, and the requisite chassis was despatched to

## BENTLEY SPEED SIX BLUE TRAIN COUPÉ
### 1930

**Top speed:** 118 mph

**Engine:** In-line 24-valve 6-cylinder

**Bore x Stroke:** 100mm x 140mm

**Capacity:** 6597cc

**Wheelbase:** 11ft 8$\frac{1}{2}$ ins (3570mm)

**Track:** 4ft 8ins (front)/4ft 8ins (rear) - 1422mm/1422mm

Gurney Nutting's coachworks in London, for a part-fabric body built on the lightweight system patented by Weymann. Barnato had sketched his requirements for what to the modern eye looks like one of the most outrageous Cad's Cars of all time. Since there was no way that adequate rear-seat headroom could be provided beneath the downswept roofline, a single sideways facing opera seat was provided there.

Gurney Nutting completed this striking three-seater early in 1930 and Barnato's idea of a test run was typical, for he took the new car thundering off to the next cross-Channel ferry, then boomed down to the South of France for a few days.

Barnato had actually been irritated

by the exaggeration of a rival company's advertisement 'Beating the Blue Train to Calais'. He pointed out that since the Blue Train ran via Marseilles, where it stopped for an hour, then to Paris, where a further three and a half hours were wasted before setting off on the final leg to Calais, there was little merit in such a claim. But driving from Cannes to London quicker than the Blue Train took to reach Calais, now that would be worthwhile.

Sharing his rakish saloon with prominent amateur golfer Dale Bourne, Barnato waited in the Carlton Bar at Cannes until 'we got word the Blue Train had left' whereupon 'we finished our drinks and left.' It was then 5.45pm. The Bentley reached

Boulogne at 10.30 next morning and the 90-minute Channel crossing to Folkestone began an hour later. They arrived in central London at 3.20 that afternoon, six minutes before the Blue Train reached Calais!

Driving the Blue Train Coupé is a memorable experience. The cabin is tiny, muscle cracking effort is necessary to steer the beast, and despite its $2\frac{1}{2}$-ton weight the $6\frac{1}{2}$-litre 6-cylinder engine provides real punch, surging effortlessly up to 60mph and beyond. The enormous drum brakes are reassuringly powerful but their hefty servo assistance demands a sensitive right foot on the pedal. But few other great cars of the 1930s can match the Blue Train Coupé for sheer presence and brooding aggression.

**ABOVE LEFT**
*Neill Bruce had particular problems photographing 'Babe' Barnato's legendary Blue Train Coupé Speed Six Bentley, simply because 'it must be the biggest car I've ever shot!' The armoured-car looks of this remarkably aggressive coupé were styled by coachbuilders J. Gurney Nutting of London.*

**ABOVE**
*The interior of the Blue Train Coupé features a unique sideways-on rear seat to exploit the maximum head- and leg-room available beneath the car's embryo 'Fastback' roofline.*

# BENTLEY S1 CONTINENTAL COUPÉ

## BENTLEY S1 CONTINENTAL COUPÉ
### 1957

**Top speed:** 120mph

**Engine:** In-line 6-cylinder

**Bore x Stroke:** 95.25mm x 114.3mm

**Capacity:** 4887cc

**Wheelbase:** 10ft 3ins (3124mm)

**Track:** 5ft 0ins (front)/5ft 0ins (rear) - 1524mm/1524mm

When the old Bentley Motor Company was absorbed by Rolls-Royce in 1931 it spelled the end of the Bentley marque as one founded squarely in motor racing. Rolls-Royce was doing more than merely buying the charisma of a five-time Le Mans 24-Hours race winner. It was buying out a potential rival, for Bentley products had been aspiring towards the upper end of the hyper-expensive quality car market. Rolls-Royce's regard for the great marque was demonstrated by their use of Bentley's distinctive Gothic arch radiator design and the winged 'B' emblem on Rolls-designed models in succeeding years.

Postwar, the more sporting luxury car owner might prefer a Bentley-radiatored and Bentley-badged Rolls-Royce to one carrying the justly revered classical radiator.
Then in 1955, Rolls-Royce launched the S-Series cars to replace the existing Mark VI and the Bentley version of this model offered – like its predecessor – a high-performance 'Continental' derivative with enhanced performance and light-weight coachwork.

The initial Series A cars had higher than standard compression 4887cc F-head power units, and the S1 was the first Bentley with automatic transmission as standard.

The Continental coachwork was created by Park Ward of London, a Rolls-Royce company since 1939, who had patented all-steel body framing as early as 1936. Their Bentley Continental bodies improved upon that by employing aluminium and light alloys throughout to save as much as 50 per cent weight.

The S-Type Continental was one of the most expensive cars in the world. Production totalled just 431 out of a total 3,475 Bentley S1s of all types manufactured between 1955 and 1958.

Beautifully-equipped, these Bentleys were not to be pressed really hard. Driven with respect the model could cram many hundreds of miles of delightful Grand Touring into an un-exhausting long day's driving. Which was the object of the exercise.

*The epitome of refined, luxurious and civilized high-speed transport, this 1957 Bentley S1 Continental once shared its motor house home with the Allard J2X pictured elsewhere in these pages.*

# BMW 3.0 CSL 'BATMOBILE'

During the 1970s, international touring car racing gained ever-increasing stature. BMW became by far the most successful of the numerous major manufacturers who supported the European Championship.

A major element in this success was the 'Big Bimmer', the 3-litre CSL two-door Coupé. According to some German sources there were three main CSL variants. The first, introduced in May 1972, used Solex carburettors on its 180bhp 3-litre 6-cylinder engine while that August saw a 3003cc version with Bosch fuel injection which achieved 200bhp. Finally, in 1973, the winged version emerged which became known as the 'Batmobile'. A minor motor racing legend – and a major one in the touring car world – had arrived.

The basic coupé model upon which the CSL was based had been introduced by BMW as a 2-litre with coachwork by Karmann as far back as 1965. The big-engined 2500 and 2800 saloons were launched into the luxury market, and a 2800CS model waved the coupé banner there, its engine quickly growing to the full 3-litre capacity.

In May 1972, BMW initiated production of the Lightweight CSL.

The last of these cars was built and sold in the aftermath of the 1973/74 Oil Crisis, when prices for any potential 'gas guzzler' bottomed. But for racing, the key to attaining ultimate performance was to minimize aerodynamic lift and drag and maximize download.

**BMW 3.0 CSL 'BATMOBILE'**
**1974**

**Top speed:** 132mph

**Engine:** In-line twin-overhead camshaft 6-cylinder

**Bore x Stroke:** 89.2mm x 80mm

**Capacity:** 3003cc

**Wheelbase:** 8ft 7$\frac{1}{4}$ins (2624mm)

**Track:** 4ft 9ins (front)/4ft 7ins (rear) -1445mm/1400mm

It was during the build up to the 1974 racing season that BMW Motorsport luminaries Jochen Neerpasch and Martin Braungart noticed the international touring car regulations which permitted evolutionary changes to existing models. This would permit them to offer the CSL for sale with aerodynamic aids, wings and spoilers. They consequently rushed a race-tuned CSL to the Stuttgart wind tunnel, where it developed some 60kg (130lbs) rear-end lift at 125mph. Helped by BMW's styling department they attached experimental wings to achieve some 70lbs download. When first tested in anger at Nürburgring circuit driver Hans-Joachim Stuck hacked nearly 15 seconds off his best time.

BMW had to offer a wing and spoiler package as standard upon a minimum homologation batch of CSLs, and this variant – complete with its eight-part attachment kit of aerodynamic aids – created such fury within the German transport authority that BMW had to pack the kit away in the car's trunk when it was sold in its native land!

**BELOW LEFT**

*During the early 1970s, BMW came to dominate not only the European Touring Car Championship with these advanced 6-cylinder fuel-injected engines but also the European Formula 2 Championship with sister 4-cylinder units. Once turbocharged in 1.5-litre form, the 4-cylinder unit won the Formula 1 World Championship title in Brabham cars driven by Nelson Piquet.*

**BELOW**

*The unmistakable profile of this 1974 BMW 3.0CSL Batmobile made the most of European touring car racing regulations by applying aerodynamic dams and wings to this rarefied batch of 'legalizing' production cars for customer sale.*

## BMW 840Ci COUPÉ

The Bavarian Motor Works unveiled its latest 8-series luxury saloon range at the Paris Salon of 1992 with the 850 CSi powered by an outstanding, state-of-the-art 5.6-litre V12 engine offering some 300bhp at 5,200rpm. The wider-appeal 840Ci model followed in the Spring of 1993, powered by a 286bhp 4-litre V8 engine.

While the V12 variant was undoubtedly exclusive and very expensive with the added cachet of being V12-powered just like the finest from Ferrari, Lamborghini and Jaguar, it was actually no faster in a straight line than the smaller-engined V8 – both 840 and 850 having a maximum (electronically-governed) of 155mph.

The smaller-engined version was fractionally faster 0-60mph, at around the 6.5sec mark, which was itself quite remarkable for such a spacious and roomy two-door coupé. The important factor was that these were extremely handsomely appointed cars in the established, rather sober and conservative BMW mode, offering more sporting character than their rivals from Mercedes-Benz 'up north' with little compromise of engineering

expertise and quality. Above all, the BMW products had an enormous wealth of recent motor sporting heritage to lean upon, and the Munich company and its dealer networks worldwide were ever eager to exploit this valuable promotional weapon, on the basis that to produce a genuine sports car, one had to be committed to the hilt in motor sport.

Into the mid-1990s, no major volume-production motor manufacturer had a better, more wide-ranging or more successful record than did 'Bay-Emm-Vay'.

---

### BMW 840Ci COUPÉ
#### 1994

**Top speed:** 155 mph

**Engine:** 90-degree four-cam 48-valve V8-cylinder

**Bore x Stroke:** 89mm x 80mm

**Capacity:** 3982cc

**Wheelbase:** 8ft 10ins (2685mm)

**Track:** 5ft 1$\frac{1}{4}$ins (front)/5ft 1$\frac{3}{4}$ins (rear) - 1554mm/1562mm

**RIGHT**
*The 840Ci Coupé expresses BMW's modern theme of cool, sober good looks while still promising enormous latent performance potential.*

**LEFT**
*BMW interiors have often been criticized as slightly too conservative. Certainly the panache of a Ferrari or Jaguar seems lacking.*

**BELOW**
*With 286bhp from its 4-litre V8 engine the rear view is all that most other road users might expect to glimpse of the 840Ci Coupé.*

# BUGATTI TYPE 57

Ettore Bugatti's legendary company, based at Molsheim in Alsace, France, introduced its Type 57 model at the Paris Salon in 1933. This was a more civilized Bugatti than before reflecting the cultured and intelligent influence of Ettore's son Jean. According to many Bugatti authorities the Type 57 should be regarded more as Jean's creation than as Ettore's even if *Le Patron* insisted upon retaining a non-detachable cylinder head design for the latest engine and completely vetoed a proposed design for an independent front suspension system.

Initially a 2.8-litre straight-eight engine had been planned but eventually a more effective 3,255cc '3.3' was adopted.

Jean Bugatti was responsible for launching the car to the dealer network and would cheerfully demonstrate Type 57s to eventual buyers visiting the factory. He was eventually relieved from these services by work's racing driver René Dreyfus who, between Grand Prix commitments, also acted as ferry driver, running new chassis from the

## BUGATTI TYPE 57 ATALANTE
### 1937

**Top speed:** 95 mph

**Engine:** In-line twin-overhead camshaft 8-cylinder (supercharged in the Type 57SC model)

**Bore x Stroke:** 72mm x 100mm

**Capacity:** 3255cc

**Wheelbase:** 10ft 10ins (3300mm)

**Track:** 4ft 5ins (front)/4ft 5ins (rear) - 1350mm/1350mm

factory to their coachbuilders, Établissements Gangloff at Colmar.

The Type 57 remained in production for five years up until the outbreak of the Second World War. Modifications made included a return to a one-piece front axle after the first cars had been recalled to re-fasten a central sleeve which had been intended to impart a small degree of independent wheel movement. Late in 1936, after some 300 cars had been produced, the engine and gearbox were fitted to the frame via rubber mounts and the chassis was stiffened with extra boxing, new cross-members

and floor supports. The rear axle was also beefed up and minor engine developments made, the original friction dampers being replaced by complex and expensive de Ram dampers. Early in 1938 Jean finally persuaded his ultra-conservative father to adopt Lockheed brakes and Allinquant tele-dampers.

But the most important single change to the series was the adoption of supercharging on the 1937 models, as the Type 57C. Where the original rigid-mounted Type 57 engines had offered some 130bhp at 4,500rpm, this figure rose with rubber mountings to

**LEFT**

*Jean Bugatti's individualistic but always well-proportioned styling signature is immediately apparent in the Midland Motor Museum's striking 1937 Bugatti Type 57 Atalante Coupé, chassis serial 57371, engine No 287.*

**ABOVE**

*During the 1930s, any enthusiast peering into this Atalante's cockpit would have been green with envy of the owner/driver. This was an enchanted place, dark, confined, full of promise... More prosaically, but no less attractive, 57371's interior, seen here, included a golf-club locker just behind the driver's door.*

**BELOW**

*Central to all Bugatti Type 57s, the straight-eight cylinder 3.3-litre engine was designed to facilitate manufacture by the Molsheim factory's relatively modest machine shop. Hand finishing enhances quality.*

135bhp and with supercharging to 160bhp at 5,000rpm. Top speed rose from 90-95mph to only 100-105mph but the major gain was in flexibility and acceleration.

Most Bugatti 57s were fitted with Jean Bugatti-designed coachwork such as the Ventoux coach (saloon), the Galibier saloon (four-door pillarless pre-1938) and the Atalante fixed-head coupé while the Aravis two-seat Cabriolet was probably Gangloff-designed.

These were expensive cars, the 1934 Atalante being priced at FF90,000, but they performed most respectably.

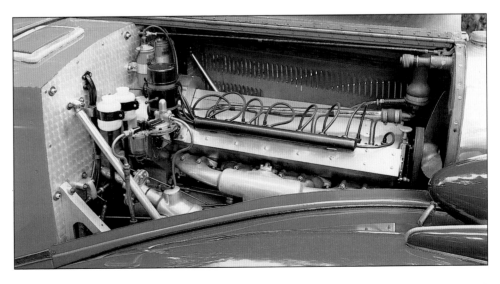

# BUGATTI EB110 GT

The original Bugatti company ceased motor manufacture in the mid-1950s upon its acquisition by the Hispano engineering group. Several devotees of the marque attempted to revive it over the following thirty years, mostly to re-create replicas of the pre-war designs, and all without conspicuous success.

But then, into the 1990s, the Italian industrialist and entrepreneur Romano Artioli suddenly appeared upon the scene announcing that he had acquired automotive rights from Hispano to manufacture under the Bugatti name. We had heard much of this before, and many observers paid little attention. However, the new Bugatti company's serious intentions were indicated by the appointment of former Lamborghini Chief Engineer Guido Stanzani to run the project, and by the establishment of a lavishly well-equipped new factory at Campogalliano, outside Modena.

Early information regarding the project emphasized that the new Bugatti Supercar would employ avant garde engineering techniques in the chassis, engine and transmission, and so it proved when the EB110 car was unveiled in September 1991, before making its International Show debut at Geneva the following March.

## BUGATTI EB110 GT
### 1993

**Top speed:** 214 mph

**Engine:** 60-degree four-cam 60-valve V12 with twin turbochargers on each cylinder bank.

**Bore x Stroke:** 81mm x 56.6mm

**Capacity:** 3498cc

**Wheelbase:** 8ft 4ins (2540mm)

**Track:** 5ft 1ins (front)/5ft 3$\frac{3}{4}$ ins (rear) - 1550mm/1620mm

The EB110 emerged as what even the fondest enthusiast could only admit was not the best-looking of two-door mid-engined coupés, powered by a 3.5-litre four-cam 60-degree V12 engine claimed to develop 560bhp at a raucous 8,000rpm. This engine featured five valves per cylinder actuated by twin overhead camshafts in each cylinder bank, and the high power output from such a modest cubic capacity was achieved thanks to twin turbochargers.

Transmission was provided by a permanently-engaged four-wheel drive system, delivering 27 per cent of its drive to the steerable front wheels, 73 per cent to the rears. The gearbox

offered six speeds, the imposing assemblage of quad-turbo V12 engine, 6-speed gearbox and four-wheel drive obviously contributing considerable weight.

Consequently, weight had to be saved in the chassis/body unit, and this was done by extensive use of ulta-light, ultra-stiff carbon-composite moulded structures, with the bodywork largely in light alloy.

The car created considerable interest, as did the lavish launch parties entertaining literally thousands of guests which were held in Paris, London and New York. The project

was dogged by public cynicism as to just how serious the new Bugatti company could be, but as time passed Artioli's empire looked secure. He even took over Lotus! And with a works-quoted top speed of 342km/h, 212mph, and a 0-60mph acceleration time around the 4sec mark, their flagship model was certainly impressive. But cabin space was criticized as being too confined. It was hot, there was little headroom for the taller driver and the controls were too heavy for most tastes. Certainly if it came to a straight contest with the off-the-peg Honda NSX, the new Bugatti seemed rather less fun to drive. Against the McLaren F1 it was no contest.

# CADILLAC V16

The Cadillac Motor Car Company of Detroit promoted itself, justifiably, as 'The Standard of the World'. Founded in 1903, it was the creation of engineer Henry M. Leland, formerly an associate of Henry Ford who had also made engines for Oldsmobile.

Leland was the American equivalent of Henry Royce, placing peerless quality and engineering excellence before expedient profit, although his company sensibly built more popularly priced cars in addition to its top-of-the-range A1-market luxury models.

His ultimate V16-cylinder design – the most complex, smoothest and finest available Cadillac – was eventually introduced in 1930 as a 7.6-litre overhead-valve engined model whose engine disposed of some 185bhp and was installed in an imposing 148-inch wheelbase chassis, capable of carrying some of the most lavish coachwork of the period.

Leland's Cadillac V16 achieved average sales of no fewer than 500 a year during its eight-season run, priced in the $6,000 – $9,000 range, in which it was joined from 1931 by an almost equally impressive V12. Power brakes were introduced that year while in 1932 ride control was applied and from 1933 'no-draught' ventilation. Dubonnet-type independent front suspension followed in 1934 and finally 'turret-top' all-steel bodies from 1935. A new short-stroke side-valve V16 eventually replaced the combined V16 and V12 models in 1938, and this definitive design would remain in production until 1940.

*Thirties splendour of epic Cecil B. De Mille proportions amply demonstrated by this florid 1930 Cadillac V16 Fleetwood Convertible. Driving one of these great monsters is akin to taking the helm of a sizeable motor launch. Having a crew of reliable lookouts helps while both motor launch and car make similar noises.*

## CADILLAC V16
### 1930

**Top speed:** 90 mph

**Engine:** 60-degree V16-cylinder

**Bore x Stroke:** 76.2mm x 101.6mm

**Capacity:** 7410cc

**Wheelbase:** 12ft 4ins (3759mm)

**Track:** 4ft 9$\frac{1}{4}$ ins (front)/4ft 11$\frac{1}{2}$ ins (rear) - 1455mm/1511mm

# CATERHAM 1700 SUPER SPRINT

Colin Chapman's Lotus Engineering Company made its name during the 1950s with a highly-sophisticated series of ultra-lightweight, supremely aerodynamically-bodied sports-racing cars which provided the launching pad for Lotus to tackle single-seater Formula 2 racing from 1957, Formula 1 from 1958 and ultimately to dominate the Formula 1 racing world for many years through the 1960s and '70s.

To help finance these wide-ranging racing interests, Lotus developed a road car line, an initial mainstay of which was the stark Lotus 7 two-seat 'fun car'. This model was marketed for many years in kit form,

for whereas a ready-assembled '7' cost £1,036 including purchase tax, the kit – exempt from purchase tax – was priced at only £536.

A prominent Lotus centre in South London was Caterham Car Services which became Britain's leading Lotus 7 specialist under the determined management of Graham Nearn. Caterham Cars began to specialize in selling used 7s, but after Lotus's own factory move from Cheshunt, North London, to Hethel, Norfolk in 1966, 7 production was compromised. Nearn then bought Lotus's float of 7 components – sufficient to build 20 complete cars – and Caterham Cars became sole U.K. distributor for the model. Eventually, in June 1973, Caterham Cars took over sole manufacturing rights to the Seven, the Lotus marque identity was dropped, and the Caterham Seven

became a model in its own right.

Caterham Sevens have since been improved and uprated over the intervening years without ever losing their distinctive Lotus Seven looks and definitive boy-racer appeal. The Lotus Big Valve Twin-Cam Ford engine was replaced by a Lotus Vegantune Twin-Cam delivering the same 126bhp but with greater mid-range torque. While a 130bhp Vegantune VTA engine offered maximum performance at one end of the Caterham range, a 1300cc Ford pushrod unit developing only 72bhp lay at the opposite extreme. The crucial factor was that in the stark, spartan and extremely lightweight Seven even 72bhp represented a high-performance power-to-weight ratio. The little cars cornered frenetically, accelerated like artillery shells, braked and steered with delightful precision and were altogether fun cars.

Caterham modified a Ford sprint engine to 100bhp and a 1600 Supersprint to 135bhp while the Cosworth BDR race-proved 16-valve 4-cylinder engine delivered 155bhp in 1600 form or 170bhp as a 1700 form endowing the Seven with performance and power-to-weight ratio akin to that of a 1961-62 Formula 1 car! The Caterham Super Seven BDR 1700 recorded 0-60mph acceleration in a blinding 5-seconds flat, 0-100mph in 18.9, and proved itself a staggering little thing to drive.

A very healthy motor racing class emerged catering solely for the Caterham products, and although their primitive aerodynamic form posed a high-drag bar to ultimate top speed it was their pace throughout the available acceleration range and cornering capabilities which made them such widely acknowledged fun to drive.

---

### CATERHAM 1700 SUPER SPRINT
#### 1990

**Top speed:** 112 mph

**Engine:** In-line 4-cylinder

**Bore x Stroke:** 83.27mm x 77.62mm

**Capacity:** 1690cc

**Wheelbase:** 7ft 4$\frac{1}{2}$ins (2250mm)

**Track:** 4ft 2ins (front)/4ft 4ins (rear) - 1270mm/1320mm

---

**ABOVE**

*New for the mid-1990s, the 2-litre 16-valve Vauxhall HPC engine in another Caterham Seven variant left photographer Bruce declaring 'a nagging feeling of a need for one!' And this despite the 1600 which he owned for a year in the mid-1980s being 'nearly impossible to drive over 50mph with the side-screens off (when it looked its best). The wind tore my glasses off my face every time I took it out!'*

**LEFT**

*The 1983 Caterham Seven 1700 Super Sprint powered by the Ford 'Kent' engine has proved itself one of the most accelerative mini-Supercars not very much money can buy. Stunningly fast up to around 120mph, but tight-fitting and spartan too!*

# CHEVROLET CORVETTE

If any design has come to be regarded as the quintessential American sports car of the 1950s and '60s, it is the Chevrolet Corvette.

The original Corvette was that great rarity, a dream car become production reality, and it was also the world's first quantity-production car to employ glassfibre moulded bodywork. It was in June 1951 that General Motors' styling chief Harley Earl briefed his design office to create an affordable American-built sports car to combat the imports from MG and Jaguar.

When the 1953 GM Motorama Show opened that January in New York's Waldorf-Astoria Hotel, Earl's 'dream car' starred, and it carried the name 'Corvette'. This styling model subsequently toured the U.S. with GM publicists estimating it was examined

*The 1954 Chevrolet Corvette was in many ways a pioneering piece, not only of automotive but of general engineering design in its adoption of moulded glassfibre bodywork which at that time was new technology – a 'plastic fantastic', no less.*

## CHEVROLET CORVETTE
### 1954

**Top speed:** 110mph

**Engine:** 90-degree V8-cylinder

**Bore x Stroke:** 98.4mm x 76.2mm

**Capacity:** 4639cc

**Wheelbase:** 8ft 6ins (2591mm)

**Track:** 4ft 9ins (front)/4ft 11ins (rear) - 1448mm/1499mm

by some 4-million people. Response was so positive that the project was cleared for production and after an initial batch of 300 Corvettes had been built in Flint, Michigan, production was moved to St. Louis, where it would run on and on until 1981.

Initially, sales were slow, and it wasn't until the arrival of the second generation Corvette in 1956 that the model really took off. Only 674 first series 'Vettes were sold in 1955 but that figure soared to 3,388 in 1956 and through the last year of the second series production, 1962, a record 14,500 were produced.

Nor was the Corvette a mere street dragster. Despite the notorious 1957 Detroit manufacturers' ban on factory or company involvement in motor racing, Chevrolet unofficially supported favoured private entries and, in 1960, a Corvette shared by John Fitch and Bob Grossman achieved a worthy 8th place in the Le Mans 24-Hours enduro, recording 150mph and more along the 3-mile Mulsanne Straight.

In national Sports Car Club of America racing, Corvettes provided the backbone of the entry within their class, and they proved capable of seeing off the Jaguar XKs and the even less wieldy Mercedes-Benz 300SLs.

But by 1962 the passage of time had caught up with the Corvette's suspension, and work began upon a Corvette replacement which ultimately emerged as the Corvette Sting Ray. But the original series 1950s 'Vette has survived with a distinctive character and charm all its own. Not the most nimble car to drive, nor a design endowed with the greatest grip and traction one might imagine, the plastic-bodied wonder in its V8 forms always had plenty of power, cornered rather more securely than one might have expected and was only really let down by its over-light and imprecise steering. But as an all-American boulevardier, with all the right looks and right sounds, the Chevrolet Corvette was a considerable success.

**ABOVE**
*The fuel-injected 290-horsepower version of GM Chevrolet Division's striking 'Vette was a rare and sought-after model, exemplified here by this well-preserved 1959 example.*

# CHEVROLET CORVETTE ZR1

Chevrolet maintained the plastic-bodied Corvette in production with all-independent suspension and four-wheel disc brakes.

For 1989 a ZF six-speed gearbox was adopted and the ultra-high performance ZR1 model, largely developed in conjunction with Lotus Engineering at Hethel in England, was launched with a 380bhp V8 engine.

This unit was an extremely advanced example of what could be done with the age-old, classical form of 90-degree American V8 power unit. Not only did the engine modifications promote what was, by emissions-regulated U.S. standards, astonishing performance, but the ZR1's chassis and running gear were also highly developed.

The ZR1's sophisticated systems extended to a computer-assisted suspension set-up, enabling the driver to adjust ride and handling qualities to his own requirements in differing circumstances. Each damper was individually equipped with a sensor/processor enabling the system to 'harden-up' as speed increased. Stages of adjustment could also be altered by the driver via a dial in the cockpit, the softest option providing a really comfortable ride while the hardest setting was described by one road tester as 'more akin to riding a glorified go-kart!'

Further modifications for 1993 endowed the advanced 5727cc engine with an output of 411bhp at a relatively lazy 5,800rpm accompanied by the most tremendous 522Nm torque at 5,200rpm.

Chevrolet Division was able to claim a maximum speed of no less than 174mph for the latest version ZR1 coupled to a 0-60mph time of around 4.3secs. But the frustrating part of all this is that if only the clock could be run back thirty years or so, all of this immense potential could have been used in the majority of American States, which is absolutely not the case in the tightly regulated, widely supervised and socially responsible 1990s.

The Chevrolet ZR1 is by some margin one of the most impressive and capable American high-performance cars ever built.

*General Motors acquired state-of-the-art European sports car technology and handling expertise by buying into Lotus Engineering in England, and one result was the magnificent Corvette ZR1; the exploitation of its full potential being, of course, illegal in every State of the Union.*

## CHEVROLET CORVETTE ZR1
### 1993

**Top speed:** 170 mph

**Engine:** 90-degree 32-valve 4-cam V8-cylinder

**Bore x Stroke:** 99mm x 93mm

**Capacity:** 5727cc

**Wheelbase:** 8ft 0$\frac{1}{4}$in (2445mm)

**Track:** 4ft 11$\frac{3}{4}$ins (front)/5ft 1in (rear) - 1465mm/1540mm

# DELOREAN

John Z. DeLorean made his name as the highly successful President of Chevrolet. But his success led him to regard himself as a guru of automotive style. He first declared plans for his 'safety sports car' as early as 1976, when it was announced that he had secured exclusive rights to a new manufacturing process and would be setting-up a production plant for the epoch-making new car in Puerto Rico. The problem was that his vision of a stainless-steel bodied, one-finish car – along the lines of Ford's Model T in the far off days when a customer could have any colour as long as it was black – was that the basic design had not been engineered for production.

DeLorean made contact with Colin Chapman's Lotus Group at Hethel in England. Financial backing had been negotiated with the British Government and a greenfield factory site at Dunmurry, outside Belfast in Northern Ireland, was quickly transformed into a major production plant.

Lotus developed the DeLorean design into a workable car in record time, the car emerging as a striking gullwing-doored coupé with a 2.8-litre fuel-injected V6 engine, produced by Renault, mounted behind the two-seat cabin, driving through a 5-speed Renault transaxle. There was an automatic option, the car rode on Lotus-developed all-independent suspension, and its unpainted stainless steel outer shell was styled by Giugiaro.

DeLorean himself had been smitten by the gullwing door feature immortalized during the mid-1950s in the Mercedes-Benz 300SL. But he either ignored or was ignorant of the problems which had always attended such a system – the impossibility of easy escape from an inverted car, the ceiling height clearance demanded within a closed garage and the mere impracticality of such doors dumping rain water straight into the seats when opened after a shower.

But DeLorean was seeking to impose his own taste upon a motoring public who were largely unimpressed with a brushed-metal finish identical to every other buyer's sister's car. Dunmurry's largely novice labour force could not be expected to match German or Japanese assembly quality straight out of the trap. U.S. customers are notoriously unforgiving and the poor quality of early DeLoreans effectively killed the project's meagre prospects.

## DELOREAN
### 1982

**Top speed:** 110 mph

**Engine:** 90-degree V6-cylinder

**Bore x Stroke:** 91mm x 73mm

**Capacity:** 2849cc

**Wheelbase:** 7ft $10^{3}/_{4}$ins ( 2406mm)

**Track -** 5ft $2^{1}/_{2}$ins (front)/5ft $2^{3}/_{8}$ins (rear) - 1590mm/1588mm

*John DeLorean's dream car project deluded British politicians, disappointed the Ulster labour force which ultimately manufactured it, and dismayed many observers of the motor industry scene on both sides of the Atlantic who had predicted disaster from its inception.*

# DODGE/ CHRYSLER VIPER RT/10

The American Chrysler Corporation stunned the automotive world with its daring release in January 1989 of a study model Dodge Viper, presenting a breathtakingly highly specified sporting car powered by an extraordinary 8-litre V10-cylinder front-mounted engine developing no less than 406bhp. This unusual and exciting power unit drove through a six-speed gearbox to the rear wheels and in response to rave reviews for the prototype Chrysler rapidly introduced the production Viper, launched in January 1992, with a GTS Coupé variant following a year later.

The Viper made a sensational impact not only within the United States but also in hitherto largely undeveloped export markets around the world. With a claimed maximum speed of 165mph and a 0-60mph time of only 4.5secs the Viper was the closest thing to a dragster that one of the giant Detroit motor manufacturing companies had ever made available for the open road.

The fact that the car's highly individualistic and quirky styling looks like a throwback to the spirit of the 1960s was no accident, but neither, unfortunately, was the appallingly bad panel fit and apparently indifferent build quality of the early cars which were appearing in Europe. The car, which on the European side of the Atlantic has to be marketed as a Chrysler since the Dodge marque name had long-since been sold to the French Renault company's commercial vehicle division, when at rest simply looked and felt like old-fashioned Detroit iron at its worst.

But out on the road the Viper's vibrant V10 engine blows away any such reservations. Whatever identifiable shortcomings in ultimate aesthetic quality there might be, the model's sheer straightline performance makes any economies seem worthwhile.

# DODGE/CHRYSLER VIPER RT/10
## 1993

**Top speed:** 190 mph

**Engine:** V10-cylinder

**Bore x Stroke:** 101.6mm x 98.55mm

**Capacity:** 7990cc

**Wheelbase:** 8ft $0\frac{1}{4}$in/2443mm

**Track:** 4ft $11\frac{1}{2}$ins (front)/5ft $0\frac{1}{2}$in (rear) - 1514mm/1540mm

Certainly, many enthusiasts have simply fallen for the car's brutish animal looks and mind-numbing acceleration. Arguably, Chrysler have developed the most extrovert Supercar to suit the most extrovert taste. So bad, many would point out, that the Viper has coiled around full circle, providing fashionable kitsch for the truly discerning!

*The staggeringly-specified Viper– sold in the U.S. as a Dodge, and in the U.K. and Europe as a Chrysler – is a genuine traffic-lights Grand Prix winner. But while the U.S.-spec car has real street mufflers each side like the Cobra 427, Eurospec demands plastic dummy mufflers instead.*

# DUESENBERG MODEL J

Perhaps the most revered of all American marques, Duesenberg was founded in competition and blossomed into exquisite maturity with a range of large, high-performance quality cars to rival the best of the Europeans.

The Duesenberg advertising slogan declared simply 'The World's Finest Motor Car', and many a lengthy and learned treatise has since been written to debate this point.

The brothers Fred and Augie Duesenberg began building passenger cars as late as 1921, the same year in which they took a team of three of their 3-litre straight-eight Indianapolis-bred racing cars to the French Grand Prix race at Le Mans where they became the first-ever non-European manufacturer to win a GP race.

Fred ensured that his prototype passenger car, the Model A, was built regardless of cost and to the highest mechanical standards. It was the first American production car to feature both a straight-eight engine and hydraulic brakes. Sadly, the Duesenberg brothers then encased their peerless mechanical designs in staid, drab bodies. The wealthy

customers of the roaring 'twenties expected better, and Duesenberg Motors went into receivership in 1926.

A majority shareholding was then taken by Errett Lobban Cord, President of the rival Auburn Automobile Company, whose startlingly florid ideas on coachwork design had already transformed Auburn's fortunes. He had also acquired Lycoming Motors, manufacturers of proprietary engines, and with Fred and Augie remaining in technical charge he merely insisted they have their engine built by

Lycoming and build their cars big, fast and startling. This was possible, with the engines delivering some 265bhp at 4,200rpm.

All bodies were to be custom-built by outside specialist coachbuilders, Duesenberg supplying only the running chassis complete with flowing fenders, bumpers, six wheels and instrument panel.

Their new Model J featured eight cylinders in-line with twin overhead camshafts operating four valves per cylinder – pure racing technology. Two standard chassis lengths were

## DUESENBERG MODEL J
### 1929

**Top speed:** 115 mph

**Engine:** In-line 8-cylinder

**Bore x Stroke:** 95.3mm x 120.7mm

**Capacity:** 6885cc

**Wheelbase:** 11ft 11$\frac{1}{2}$ins (3644mm)

**Track -** 5ft 2$\frac{1}{2}$ins (front)/5ft 0ins (rear) - 1588mm/1524mm made, 142½ ins ('short'!) or 153½ ins (long) while a solitary 'J Car' with an enormous 178-inch wheelbase supported the landaulette 'Throne Car' bodywork for the evangelist 'Father Divine'.

Each of these chassis was tested for 500 miles around the Indianapolis Motor Speedway before passing to its coachbuilder. The J's strength and longevity would become legendary, and its finish equalled the finest of European imports. In 1932 the supercharged Model SJ emerged while two 125-inch wheelbase SSJ 'short

supercharged' cars were also made to special order.

The J chassis was popular with coachbuilders since it was so long, low and rigid, but Duesenberg created the styling designs which the coach-builders were licensed to use. From 1929 – 31 Gordon Buehrig became Chief Designer. Nearly one third of all Js and SJs were bodied by the Walter M. Murphy Company of Pasadena, while Bohman & Schwarz proved the next most popular. The Duesenberg marque finally died with the collapse of the Cord Corporation in August

1937, although the last SJ of only some 480 J-series cars built, was finally completed in 1938. From that day forward Duesenberg has survived in popular acclaim as the greatest of all great American automotive classics.

*The epitome of the great American automotive dream between the two World Wars, the Duesenberg Model J, provided presence, beauty, fine quality and immense prestige for the wealthy owner. It was powered by nothing more than a proprietary Lycoming engine – but it proved good enough.*

# FERRARI 500 SUPERFAST

The Superfast was the Maranello marque's equivalent of the Bugatti Royale – the largest, the most luxurious, the most expensive – simply the most lavish and most opulent. It was a high-performance rocket ship in the Pullman mould, and when the first metallic blue prototype was unveiled at the Geneva Salon of March 1964, it was unchallengeably the finest touring Ferrari yet.

The Superfast was powered by a custom-made version of Ferrari's legendary V12-cylinder engine, one of

proportion. The bodies were built with special care in Turin, while Maranello assembled its 500 Superfasts in two distinct groups, the first of some 25 vehicles and the second – featuring newly-introduced five-speed all-synchromesh gearboxes in place of the previous four-speed with overdrive – comprising only twelve.

The only external difference between the two Series was a three-vent side panel introduced on the Series II versions high behind each front-wheel arch, where it replaced the Series I's eleven-louvre panel. The Maranello factory turned out Superfasts at the rate of approximately one a month and all but six of the first Series and one of the second had left-hand drive, the

ponderous overhangs and inadequate ventilation. The standards by which one judged a Supercar in the 1960s have changed tremendously into the 1990s.

**BELOW**

*Arguably the most beautiful of all Maranello's big-engined Supercars, the 5-litre V12-engined Ferrari 500 Superfast combined wonderfully well-proportioned good looks (by Pininfarina) with real performance, power, and comfort. This is chassis '6673'.*

**RIGHT**

*This convertible Ferrari 275GTS (Spider) is unusual in featuring a 2+1 seating arrangement. The charismatic open Spiders are rarer and generally more valuable in market terms than closed road-going GTs.*

their 'long-block' units with detachable cylinder heads. Its capacity was just under 5-litres and it was rated at no less than 400bhp at 6,500rpm.

Pininfarina's *aerodinamica* body style for the Superfast was a stunning contemporary exercise in grace and

exceptions featuring right-hand drive for the enthusiastic British market.

The Superfast today remains every bit as opulent and lavishly equipped and furnished as in its heyday, but it is typically front-engined V12 touring Ferrari in its heavy controls,

---

### FERRARI 500 SUPERFAST
#### 1965

**Top speed:** 170 mph

**Engine:** 60-degree two-cam V12-cylinder

**Bore x Stroke:** 88mm x 68mm

**Capacity:** 4961cc

**Wheelbase -** 8ft 8ins/2650mm

**Track:** 4ft 7½ins (front)/4ft 7ins (rear) - 1404mm/1397mm

# FERRARI 275 GTB

The 3.3-litre V12 front-engined Ferrari 275GTB and its open sister, the 275GTS, were launched simultaneously to a wildly enthusiastic reception at the Paris Salon of 1964. The twin models shared a common chassis and a common engine design, and the models were intended to replace the lovely 250GT *Lusso* which had become established as the absolute epitome of production Italian Supercar design – Pininfarina styling at its magnificently proportioned best.

The new GTB was intended to offer far more sporting potential than the strictly touring *Lusso*. The two-cam engine was bored out from the 250 model's 3-litres to 3,285cc. In initial form with three Weber carburettors this latest Ferrari V12 produced 280bhp at 7,600rpm, while the alternative six-carburettor option offered a full 300bhp which guaranteed explosive performance.

The GTB then introduced independent rear suspension to the Ferrari line, replacing the live axle of preceding Maranello designs, while a rear-mounted five-speed transaxle transmission was also adopted to improve weight distribution in favour of improved handling and cornering power. Brakes were never ideal.

The clutch remained in unit with the engine up front, while early-series cars employed a slender propeller shaft driving to the rear-mounted transaxle supported by a steady-bearing amidships. Later cars featured a torque tube enclosing the prop shaft to link clutch housing and transaxle in a rigidly integrated assembly extending beneath the car's cabin.

The GTB bodyshell was another highly successful co-production between stylist Carrozzeria Pininfarina and manufacturer Carrozzeria Scaglietti. Produced initially in 'shortnose' form, an improved 'longnose' was subsequently introduced for aerodynamic reasons.

**LEFT**
*Interiors of all the mid-'60s Pininfarina-styled Ferrari road cars combined leather-trimmed opulence with practicality. This is the cabin of the 275 GBT 'Longnose' below.*

**BELOW**
*The 1966 Ferrari 275GTB 'Longnose' was perhaps the pick of the Maranello bunch for overall performance, handling and consistent cornering power, its lengthened nose enhancing aerodynamic balance.*

**RIGHT**
*Power unit of the 275GTB was a 3.3-litre V12 available in either two or 4-cam, triple or six-carburettor, configuration.*

## FERRARI 275 GTB
### 1966

**Top speed:** 155 mph

**Engine:** 60-degree two-cam V12-cylinder – four-cam option available as the 275GTB/4

**Bore x Stroke:** 77mm x 58.8mm

**Capacity:** 3285cc

**Wheelbase:** 7ft $10^{1/2}$ins (2400mm)

**Track:** 4ft 6ins (front)/4ft 7ins (rear) - 1377mm/1393mm

# FERRARI 365 GTB/4 DAYTONA

One of the last of the truly great front-engined Supercars, the Ferrari Daytona was unveiled at the Paris Salon of October 1968, whereupon it became simultaneously both the most expensive and the fastest (174mph) road car to have been produced in the Ferrari marque's then 21-year history.

Why Daytona? The Italians' use of the famous Floridan racing and records venue's name dates from Ford's first victory over Ferrari in the Le Mans 24-Hours race of 1966, when the victorious trio of Ford Mark II cars had rumbled across the finish line in arrow-head formation after all the significant Ferraris had broken. At Maranello Mr. Ferrari exhorted his engineers and drivers to try harder. With extra funding from Fiat for 1967 they had responded with the Ferrari 330P4 prototypes, two of which headed a Ferrari 1-2-3 revenge victory over Ford in the Daytona 24-Hour race of February 1967, culminating in the blood-red Ferraris yowling over the finish line three-abreast after the Fords had faltered. To the Italian racing world revenge had never been so sweet and the new front-engined Ferrari 365GTB/4 took the name in due homage.

## FERRARI 365 GTB/4 DAYTONA
### 1971

**Top speed:** 172 mph

**Engine:** 60-degree four-cam V12-cylinder

**Bore x Stroke:** 81mm x 71mm

**Capacity:** 4390cc

**Wheelbase:** 7ft 10$\frac{1}{2}$ins (2400mm)

**Track:** 4ft 8$\frac{3}{4}$ins (front)/4ft 8ins (rear) - 1441mm/1422mm

**ABOVE**
*Most sought-after and historic of all the Ferrari 365GTB/4 Daytona series are the rarefied batches of pure-blood racing competizione versions. This one is ex-Col. Ronnie Hoare's renowned British Maranello Concessionaires team.*

**LEFT**
*Only seven right-hand drive 365GTS/4 Daytona Spiders were produced by Ferrari, chassis serials 14371 and '373, 15841, '909, '917, '963 and '969. Any others were converted from left-hand drive originals or cut down from closed Berlinettas.*

But the new Daytona was not only fast along the straight. The spacious and typically hefty, but delightful, two-door Berlinetta was also timed through the standing-start quarter-mile in only 13.8 secs and it crossed the timing line at 107.5mph – just 440 yards after blast-off. Its 0-60mph time was a mere 5.9secs, shattering by 1969-70 standards.

While the essence of the Daytona's appeal was its Leonardo Fioruavanti-styled coachwork, its heart was the 4.4-litre four-cam V12 engine which breathed through a parade of six twin-choke Weber downdraught carburettors marching up the valley of the vee and which developed no fewer than 352bhp at a raucous, indeed spine-tingling, 7,500rpm.

Transmission was via a five-speed manual transmission, with the standard Ferrari long one-arm bandit lever shift and precise, if slow, clack-clack shift movement.

While the prototype cars had been styled, and its bodywork also built by Pininfarina in Turin, the essentially steel bodyshells were subsequently put into production by Scaglietti in Modena, close by the Maranello assembly plant. Some weight was saved by adoption of aluminium opening panels (doors, bonnet, trunklid), and further lightened series of pure competition Daytonas were also produced specifically for the *Gran Turismo* category at Le Mans and in similar endurance events.

# FERRARI F40

Enzo Ferrari's magical marque made its debut in 1947, and as the 40th anniversary of this happy event approached in 1987 he and his manufacturing partner, Fiat, which owned the production side of the Ferrari empire, decided to celebrate the occasion in a practical way by introducing a limited-production Supercar which would set new standards, not only as the fastest road-going Ferrari yet, but as a contender for the title 'The World's Fastest'.

In effect, the F40 was a contemporary Group B racer clad in roadgoing clothes. It was announced that no more than 450 were to be built over the following 30 months, sales to be allocated to selected clients only. In fact, many more were necessary to fulfil clamorous demand. Based upon a conventional steel frame, the F40 made extensive use of carbon-composite moulded panels bonded structurally to the steel chassis elements.

**TOP LEFT**

*0–200mph starts here! The Ferrari F40's twin-turbo V8 engine bay is dominated by coolers and gas piping. This particular example features exhaust-emission control catalytic converters and adjustable suspension, given away by those hydraulic pipes attached to the rear shocks.*

**BELOW LEFT**

*Ferrari's epic F40 was introduced in celebration of the marque's 40th anniversary, in 1987, powered by twin-turbocharged V8 engine to prove itself at that time the world's fastest production Supercar. This is Maranello Concessionaires' 1988 pre-production prototype, chassis 77289, with sliding perspex side windows.*

**ABOVE RIGHT**

*Startling rear three-quarter aspect of the Ferrari F40 reflects its uncompromising adoption of purebred modern motor racing technology.*

**BELOW**

*The Ferrari 'Evolution 288' Supercar variant which built towards the F40, pictured here at the 1993 Goodwood Festival of Speed.*

Central to this startling new two-seat coupé was its light-alloy block V8 engine which was similar to that employed in the recently-launched Ferrari 288GTO but was now revised with different bore/stroke dimensions to displace 3-litres. The engine was equipped with twin turbocharging which meant that this capacity – when multiplied by the equivalency factor which the racing authorities employed to equalize performance between turbocharged and atmospheric-induction engines – fell just within the notional 5-litre ceiling in that category.

Upon its launch the F40 was viewed very much as a potential rival to Porsche's four-wheel drive 959, and in performance terms the Italian challenger was certainly a potent threat – 0-124mph acceleration being claimed as 12.0 secs and top speed no less than 201.3mph!

Twin Japanese-made IHI turbochargers were specified to boost Weber/Marelli electronic injection and engine management which was similar to the system employed on Ferrari's contemporary Formula 1 racing cars.

But the F40 engine thundered out – or rather, with its turbochargers muffling the exhaust note, whuffled out – no fewer than 478bhp at 7,000rpm which made it easily one of the most powerful 'road' cars ever unleashed for public sale.

It rode on 17-inch diameter wheels – 13-inches wide at the driven rear end and wore Pirelli P700 tyres. Bag-type safety fuel tanks with foam filling carried some 26 (imperial) gallons and the car's coil-and-wishbone suspension featured a speed-sensitive adjustment system which dropped the car 20mm to achieve optimum aerodynamic form, and raised it 20mm for practical manoeuvring at low speed, kerb clearance, etc.

Pininfarina had cooperated with the Ferrari factory body engineers and aerodynamicists to perfect what rapidly proved itself to be by far the most exciting Supercar built until that time, and one which for sheer adrenalin-pumping excitement left the altogether better-finished and far more sophisticated German Porsche 959 seriously overshadowed.

For here was a car which breathed uncompromising function from every lightweight, racebred pore – sheer animal performance being the prime objective rather than finish and fancy looks for main-square posing. The F40 was certainly Ferrari's finest, and a really Super car. But it also deserved to be treated with respect. It was not a car for the unwise or unwary to attempt to drive rapidly. It was a genuine wolf in wolf's clothing.

---

### FERRARI F40
#### 1991

**Top speed:** 220 mph

**Engine:** 90-degree V8-cylinder

**Bore x Stroke:** 82mm x 69.5mm

**Capacity:** 2936cc

**Wheelbase:** 8ft $0\frac{1}{2}$in (2451mm)

**Track:** 5ft $2\frac{3}{4}$ins (front)/5ft $3\frac{1}{2}$ins (rear) - 1595mm/1610mm

---

# FERRARI 456 GT

This front-engined Ferrari is the latest and most expensive flagship of the legendary Italian marque's modern range, powered by a 5.5-litre V12 engine driving through a 6-speed transaxle mounted in unit with the final-drive at the rear of the car. It was greeted with considerable acclaim upon its public unveiling at the Paris Salon of 1992, being ostensibly a thoroughly modern example of the kind of thoroughbred breeding which had previously produced the large and luxurious 412 high-performance saloon. However, the 456 GT has also attracted some criticism for the Pininfarina-styled coachwork's almost uncanny resemblance from certain angles to a far less august and costly body style by Toyota of Japan! More 'Supracar' than 'Supercar', perhaps?

While any such criticism is obviously complete anathema to the dedicated *Ferrarista* it has to be said that this kind of look-alike similarity between some of the world's most expensive and lavishly equipped cars and the far more affordable products of the mass-production industry has become inevitable in recent years, as features which were once confined purely to the realms of the Supercar

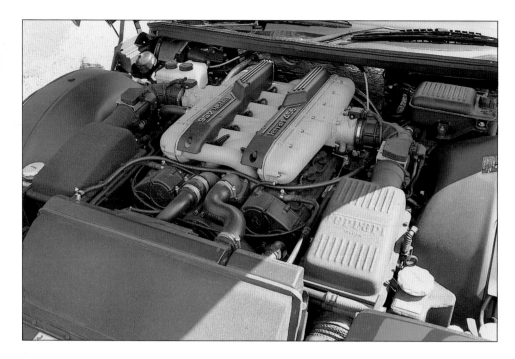

## FERRARI 456 GT
### 1994

**Top speed:** 188 mph

**Engine:** 60-degree two-cam V12-cylinder – four-cam option available as the 275GTB/4

**Bore x Stroke:** 77mm x 58.8mm

**Capacity:** 3285cc

**Wheelbase:** 7ft 10$\frac{1}{2}$ins (2400mm)

**Track** - 4ft 7$\frac{1}{2}$ins (front)/4ft 7$\frac{3}{4}$ins (rear) - 1409mm/1416mm

now feature upon many mass-produced off-the-peg sporting cars.

At the heart of the unobtrusively fast and plainly immensely capable 456 GT is the latest V12 engine itself which now has a 65-degree vee angle replacing the traditional 60-degree valley to decrease overall unit height and so permit the bonnet line to be substantially lower than its predecessors.

The engine is a four-cam with four valves per cylinder, seven main bearings and dry-sump lubrication. It is a fuel-injected, electronically-managed unit developing no less than 442bhp at only 6,250rpm – a remarkably lazy level by traditional Ferrari standards. The factory claims a maximum speed of 189mph matched by a 0-60mph time of around 5 secs. Despite its allegedly

Japanese appearance it is not only a handsome and soberly well-appointed projectile but a very pleasant and civilized machine from the point of view of both driver and passenger.

**TOP LEFT**
*The 65-degree V12 power unit of the ultra-modern 456 GT nestles deep beneath its heat shields and cowls, 442bhp is here.*

**BELOW LEFT**
*Interior of the British-market Ferrari 456 GT demonstrator operated by Ferrari U.K. In its furnishing, fixtures and fittings the 456 GT strikes a sober balance between opulence, comfort and practicality.*

**ABOVE**
*Maranello's highly civilized and well-appointed limousine for the 1990s, the shapely Ferrari 456 GT, demonstrates Pininfarina styling at its most modern. But Toyota, for example, had already produced similar shapes which are rather more affordable. What would have been Supercars in the 1970s and '80s are being mass-produced in the 1990s.*

# FORD GT40

One of the most sensational road cars of the 1960s had its beginnings in Henry Ford II's ambition to win some of the sporting world's truly classic races. In 1962 he invested his company's vast resources in a campaign which would ultimately bring victory in the Indianapolis 500-Miles speedway classic, in countless international rallies and ultimately in the greatest single road racing event of them all, the Le Mans 24-Hours.

He had tried to ease Ford's way into the sporting world by attempting to take over the established multiple-World Champion race-winning marque of Ferrari in Italy, but Mr. Ferrari refused and Henry Ford II privately vowed to beat Ferrari at his own game. Ford Advanced Vehicles Operations was established in England and the accomplished and established British designer and racing car manufacturer Eric Broadley of Lola Cars Ltd. was contracted since he had already run a Ford V8-powered, mid-engined coupé at Le Mans in 1963.

That Lola GT design was effectively reworked to alter the emphasis from its being an aluminium-hulled monocoque-chassised pure competition coupé to becoming a steel-monocoque semi-production coupé of raceable performance. The initially 4.2-litre V8-powered Ford GT then made its competition debut – unsuccessfully – in 1964 when its computer-assisted design proved itself very fast indeed but aerodynamically unstable and with suspect reliability.

Ford quickly learned that simply throwing dollars at the problem provided no guarantee of success. The top executives in Detroit had badly misjudged the size of the problem and the strength of the established opposition, but disappointments through 1964-65 were speedily overcome.

The 4.2-litre V8 engines rapidly made way for 4.7s and ultimately 5-litre and 7-litre versions, and while the 4.7 and 5-litre cars formed the backbone of production Ford GT40 manufacture, it was the 7-litre Mark II and later Mark IV cars which ultimately won Le Mans for Ford in 1966 and 1967. A change in regulations then saw a 5-litre ceiling applied to racing 'Sports' cars and the Gulf-JW Automotive racing team's famous powder-blue and orange-liveried 5.0 GT40s won Le Mans twice more, with the self-same individual GT40 chassis '1075', in both 1968 and 1969.

The GT40 was an immensely enjoyable car to drive, staggeringly

quick by contemporary standards. It could accelerate from 0-100mph in 12secs, and properly geared would top the magic 200mph, all on an ordinary old iron Ford V8 pushrod engine. It was certainly one of the last Le Mans-winning cars one could happily and practically use on the public road.

**ABOVE AND BELOW**

*The legendary GT40, built by Ford Advanced Vehicles at Slough, England, was ultimately to win two Le Mans 24-Hour races and the World Championship endurance racing title. Here we see the mid-engined race-bred coupé lines of its moulded glass fibre bodywork and rear-mounted V8 engine.*

## FORD GT 40
### 1965

**Top speed:** 210 mph

**Engine:** 90-degree V8-cylinder

**Bore x Stroke:** 101.6mm x 72.9mm (initial production 4.7-litre)

**Capacity:** 4736cc

**Wheelbase:** 7ft 11ins (2413mm)

**Track:** 4ft 6ins (front)/4ft 8ins (rear) - 1371mm/1422mm

# FORD MUSTANG

Ford's Mustang series effectively took a leaf out of Jaguar's book by offering more horsepower and miles per hour per dollar than almost any other manufacturers before or since. It was not a car of unusual design, but a car of unusual public appeal.

The Mustang was officially introduced in April 1964 and it provided one of the most stunning automobile success stories of modern time. Within five months it had become the third most popular model in the U.S. beaten only by the full-sized Chevrolet and Ford. Over 400,000 Mustangs were sold in its first sales year and in 1965 well over half a million were purchased.

The Mustang was the result of almost ten years of Ford research and development. Research was not merely technical, it also delved deep into marketing priorities and identified the moneyed new youth market. Ford's first postwar 'sporty' car had been the Thunderbird of 1954-58 but its demise in favour of a much larger model left only one two-seater car on the USW list – Chevrolet's Corvette.

Early in 1961 Ford began to research the 'personal car' field and within a year experimental designs began to emerge. The top secret styling department produced one study under the code-name 'Median' which offered a long nose line and four-seat accommodation.

A show car was then produced to gauge public reaction under the name Mustang I. It was absolutely not a production prototype, featuring a hand-made multi-tubular steel frame and stressed aluminium skinned body. It was also mid-engined, with a German Ford Taunus V4 power unit behind the cockpit, a faired roll-over bar behind the cockpit and fold-away concealed headlamps.

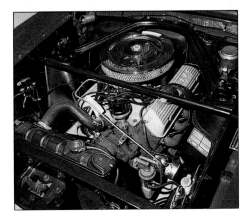

**ABOVE**
*Ford's wonderfully versatile series of 90-degree V8 iron-block engines powered everything from Le Mans 24-Hours and Indianapolis '500' winners to the Shelby GT350, as seen here.*
**BELOW**
*Biggest of the Shelby American 'muscle car' range was the deep-chested GT500.*

Meanwhile, the marketeers had settled upon a requirement for a four-seat production Mustang, a prototype Mustang II appearing at the United States GP meeting, Watkins Glen, N.Y., in 1963. This had the correct wheelbase and track and a 289 cubic inch 271bhp Ford V8 engine.

Lee Iacocca forced it through. The Mustang was launched in four basic body forms, a hard-top coupé, two-door sedan with no pillar between front and rear windows; a convertible and a true 2-plus-2 fastback coupé. Less than 200lbs separated the weight difference between the cars. A choice of either in-line 6-cylinder or V8 engines was offered, the 289 cubic inch V8 offering as much as 385bhp tuned with Weber carburation. The 6-cylinders were 170 cubic inch growing to 200, while both manual and automatic transmissions were available.

Drum brakes were standard on Mustangs, with front discs an optional extra. While the 289 V8 engine was adopted from 1962 by Carroll Shelby for his AC Ace-derived Cobra sports cars, Shelby American Inc. also arranged with Ford to produce a special run of lightened, Cobra-Ford engined Mustangs known as the Shelby GT350. Only Fastbacks were presented and the GT500 followed with full 427 cubic inch (7-litre) V8 engine.

**FORD MUSTANG**
**1965**

**Top speed:** 120 mph

**Engine:** 90-degree V8-cylinder

**Bore x Stroke:** 101.6mm x 72.9mm (4.7-litre)

**Capacity:** 4736cc

**Wheelbase:** 9ft 0ins (2743mm)

**Track:** 4ft 10ins (front)/4ft 10ins (rear) - 1473mm/1473mm

# FRAZER NASH LE MANS REPLICA

The BMW 328 6-cylinder 2-litre engine was a jewel of 1930s design and in 1945, when German industry lay devastated, the Bristol Aeroplane Company in England took on the design as part war reparation. Through AFN Ltd., pre-war manufacturers of Frazer Nash cars and importers of the BMW, they retained the services of BMW designer Dr Fritz Fiedler.

The first Bristol car, the 400 model, emerged in 1946, using the 328 frame and power unit virtually unchanged but clothed in aerodynamic bodywork.

H.J. Aldington of AFN Ltd. used the same engine for his postwar sports cars, the first emerging in 1948 as the 120bhp 'Speed Model'. One of these cars, slightly modified, finished third in the Le Mans 24-Hours race of 1949, and the always commercially-minded 'HJ' promptly marketed versions as the Frazer Nash 'Le Mans Replica'.

During 1950, the Le Mans Rep invariably dominated the 2-litre class in sports car competition wherever it appeared. In Sicily Franco Cortese – the first man ever to drive a Ferrari in racing – ran second for Frazer Nash in the Targa Florio classic, and finished

6th in the Mille Miglia with the same car. Back again for the 1952 Targa Florio he won the great race outright.

Meanwhile, American customer Stuart Donaldson entered a car for Harry Grey and Larry Kulok in the Sebring 12-Hours – America's most important enduro race – and they won!

In 1952, a Mark II version was introduced with reduced frontal area, lower weight and improved road holding. Some 60 Le Mans Replicas were made in all.

Imagine yourself sitting virtually on the floor in that high cockpit, with the barrel-shaped body rolling around your legs, those cycle mudguards in clear view each side, feet stretched out virtually straight ahead to the pedals and large-diameter thin-rimmed steering wheel grasped in your palms. There's a lengthy cranked gearshift by your left hand, and that smooth, willing Bristol engine is just raring to go. And go it does, up to 120bhp at 5,500rpm, the standing-start quarter-mile in around 16secs, and a top speed

of 120mph or more.

Make no mistake, the Frazer Nash Le Mans Rep is a truly great classic car – its reputation is justly deserved.

**TOP AND ABOVE**
*When Norman Culpan and H.J. Aldington, guiding hand behind AFN Ltd., manufacturers of Frazer Nash sports cars, finished third in the 1949 Le Mans 24-Hour race, their High Speed model became the prototype for the Le Mans Replica cars which followed. This splendid example has been preserved in England's Midland Motor Museum.*

## FRAZER NASH LE MANS REPLICA
### 1950

**Top speed:** 120 mph

**Engine:** In-line 6-cylinder

**Bore x Stroke:** 66mm x 96mm

**Capacity:** 1971cc

**Wheelbase:** 8ft 0ins (2438mm)

**Track:** 4ft 0ins (front)/4ft 2ins (rear) - 1371mm/1422mm

# HONDA NSX

As the Japanese motor industry flexed its immense muscle and came to command the motoring markets of the developed world, it became something of a truism to say 'Yeah but – the Japanese can't build decent sports cars...'

For many years that tended to be true. The corporate Japanese conception of sporting motoring always seemed to fall short of the best European standards, until, that is, Honda launched their affordable off-the-peg Supercar, the NSX.

This quite remarkable mid-engined two-seat coupé was unveiled in prototype form in Chicago, U.S.A. in February 1989, production then being initiated for the 1990 model year.

The basis of the NSX was a well-developed and well-packaged aluminium chassis/body structure with its 90-degree V6-cylinder 3-litre power unit mounted behind the cabin, driving through a five-speed transaxle to the rear wheels. The engine featured twin overhead camshafts upon each cylinder bank, actuating four valves per cylinder, and with the latest state-of-the-art electronic engine management and fuel injection the NSX was endowed with around 274bhp at 7,300rpm.

## HONDA NSX
### 1993

**Top speed:** 167 mph

**Engine:** 60-degree 24-valve four-cam V6-cylinder

**Bore x Stroke:** 90mm x 78mm

**Capacity:** 2977cc

**Wheelbase:** 8ft 4ins (2530mm)

**Track:** 4ft 11 ins (front)/5ft 0ins (rear) - 1510mm/1530mm

What so impressed NSX drivers world-wide was the Honda's wonderfully predictable handling, its well-balanced, precise and direct steering, typically Japanese good finish and particularly its fine gearchange.

Paradoxically, while the mid-engined layout with engine behind the cabin but ahead of the rear axle line is plainly the most effective in promoting a well balanced and good-handling high-performance car, its main disadvantage is the lengthy gear-change run then left between the driver's shift lever and the transaxle hanging out behind in the car's tail.

Lamborghini avoided such problems by placing the gearbox in the cabin area, by the driver's hip, and then accepted the powertrain inefficiencies introduced by the need to reverse drive direction back through the engine to the rear wheels. Honda simply applied intelligent lateral thinking to providing a cable change shift with decent control and minimum 'slop' or lost movement.

The result was what became an industry standard for gearchanging excellence, and this feature alone helped elevate the NSX onto a pedestal all of its own – until the McLaren F1 came along.

**TOP AND ABOVE**
*The Honda NSX set entirely new standards in so-called Supercar ride, handling, gearchange and driveability and raised the level of the game. McLaren took it as their starting point for the F1 project. The 24-valve V6 engine unobtrusively produced around 274 bhp.*

# INVICTA
# S-TYPE

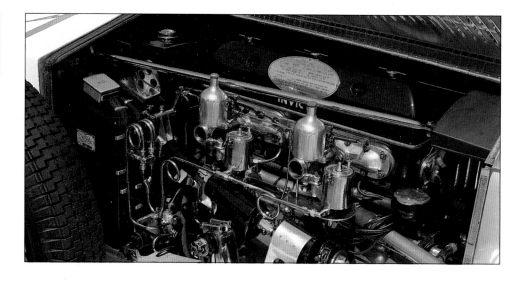

Invicta Cars was a well-founded company, in that Captain Noel Macklin and his business partner Earl Fitzwilliam put considerable capital into the concern's launch in 1925. The first production Invictas were powered by 3-litre proprietary Meadows engines and they proved themselves to be pleasant, if not particularly outstanding, fast tourers. Miss Violet Cordery did promotional wonders for the marque by driving one of these cars round the world but the really sporting Invicta was the 4$\frac{1}{2}$-litre which Captain Macklin introduced in 1928 and which used the 6-cylinder Meadows engine also made famous – ultimately as a Le Mans 24-Hour race winning unit – by Lagonda.

The Meadows engine's power output, of around 110bhp, in addition to its iron-block weight, proved rather too much for what was basically the original Invicta 3-litre chassis, and for 1929 a redesigned chassis was introduced with lowered radiator to carry improved Meadows engines.

In September 1930, Invicta's first '100mph' chassis was introduced, part-engineered by the famous rally specialist Donald Healey, and a real attempt was made to provide road-holding more in keeping with its performance.

The leafsprings were flattened and underslung and the revised model's overall centre of gravity substantially lowered. A much lower radiator and scuttle line was adopted and these cars certainly became capable of a true 90mph, and could trim 100 under favourable conditions.

These Invictas then gained a somewhat dubious reputation for handling and as rather heavy and inflexibly sprung cars with most of their weight on the front axle they were certainly a handful. But as long as the driver made suitable allowances, they had the advantage for sheer performance and a competition record including team

prizes in the important Alpine Trial; fastest time of the day on many of the difficult passes was capped by Healey winning the 1931 Alpine Rally. In 1932 when production ceased, around 80 had been produced.

*Sir Noel Macklin's Invicta marque is best remembered today for the rakish low-chassis S-Type such as Nigel Dawes' much-loved example seen here. Its 4½-litre 6-cylinder Meadows engine was one of the most popular (and best) proprietary power units of the 1930s.*

## INVICTA S-TYPE
### 1932

**Top speed:** 100 mph

**Engine:** In-line 6-cylinder

**Bore x Stroke:** 88.5mm x 120.64mm

**Capacity:** 4467cc

**Wheelbase:** 9ft 10ins (2997mm)

**Track:** 4ft 8ins (front)/4ft 8ins (rear) - 1473mm/1473mm

# JAGUAR XK150

The immortal Jaguar XK series of production sports cars was manufactured in Coventry, England, from 1948 to 1961. During that period they set new standards of value-for-money performance, technical specification and sheer, simple grace. The range embraced three major models – the original XK120 being succeeded by the XK140 (from 1954) and finally the XK150 (from 1957).

Jaguar's in-line 6-cylinder twin-overhead camshaft power unit provided the 'XK' part of the model name, while the '120' part of the initial model's name related to its claimed maximum speed, 120mph. This does not apply, however, where the later replacements are concerned. For the XK140 and XK150 merely reflect major revision in the basic design's production specification, not major hikes in their maximum speed potential.

William Lyons had founded his business, the Swallow Sidecar manufacturing works in Blackpool, Lancashire, in 1922. He became a highly regarded stylist and coachbuilder, eventually producing a series of very attractive special bodies for such mainstream manufacturers as Austin and Riley. In fact it was to be closer to their production plants that he moved his business to Coventry and with William Heynes (ex-Humber) as his Chief Engineer, began to build cars under the SS name, using engines made by the Standard Motor Co.

During the Second World War, Lyons prompted Heynes to plan for the future, and what became the formidably successful series of 'XK' 6-cylinder twin-cam engines was conceived during fire-watching duty protecting the Foleshill, Coventry factory from German air-raid damage.

With Claude Baily and Walter Hassan as his co-designers, Heynes laid out the engine initially as a 3.2-litre but when low-speed torque proved inadequate the stroke was increased, to achieve a definitive 3442cc. Meanwhile, wartime activities of the German SS had rendered the name unsuitable, and William Lyons renamed his company Jaguar Cars.

A subsidiary 2-litre 4-cylinder 'XJ' 100 model was planned but when the 3.4-litre prototype Jaguar XK120 was launched at the 1948 London Motor Show, orders were so immense that Jaguar Cars found itself unable to meet demand and the '100' was shelved.

The new XK120's box-section steel chassis was a real heavyweight, its independent front suspension featured wishbones and torsion bars while the live rear axle was on semi-elliptic leafsprings. Lyons had initially planned to build no more than 200 of the sports cars to test the engine in public before the final objective, a new saloon car range, could be launched. But almost immediately the export order book, especially from the U.S.A., was so jam-packed that a full production programme was laid down for the 120.

The first 200-odd cars were aluminium-bodied over wooden frames, but full production then took over with steel body pressings from the Pressed Steel Company. The first export XK120s went to the U.S.A. in 1949 and a steady flow began in 1950.

The XK120 soon began racing, and the 'C-Type' competition variant – actually a very different car powered by that same wonderful engine – won the Le Mans 24-Hours classic in both 1951 and 1953.

By 1954, when the replacement XK140 was introduced, over 12,000 XK120s had been built in roadster, drophead coupé and coupé variants. The XK140 offered the same three body alternatives, the standard engine now offering 190bhp and the special-equipment, with C-Type cylinder head, 210bhp. Rack-and-pinion steering made the car far more predictable, and weight distribution was improved by moving the engine further forward and placing the battery ahead of the bulkhead instead of behind the seats.

## JAGUAR XK150
### 1959

**Top speed:** 125 mph

**Engine:** In-line twin-overhead camshaft 6-cylinder

**Bore x Stroke:** 83mm x 106mm

**Capacity:** 3442cc

**Wheelbase:** 8ft 6ins (2590mm)

**Track:** 4ft 3¼ins (front)/4ft 3¼ins (rear) - 1301mm/1301mm

By 1957, separate-chassis cars with add-on coachwork were obsolescent technology, unitary construction chassis/body design being the new and more cost-effective norm. The XK150 therefore emerged as a more refined sporting Jaguar pending arrival of the unitary-construction E-Type. It had a more roomy cockpit and the roadster became Jaguar's first to offer wind-up windows and Borg Warner automatic transmission, as on later 140s. The 150 had a higher scuttle, but featured C-Type proven disc brakes on all four wheels, still a novelty in 1957. In 1958 the XK150S was launched, 250bhp initially for export only, with three 2-inch SU carburettors as would be adopted on the later E-Type and Mark X saloon.

On the road the XK Jaguars were in truth rather ponderous though undeniably fast. The pre-disc brake models, in inexperienced hands in particular, could be seen as the potential cause of an accident looking for somewhere to happen. The Moss gearbox was always a weak point, with a baulky and indeterminate shift, and for many the driving position was confined and uncomfortable. But as a proper sports car of the classic period a decent driver could wring some tremendous motoring out of it. The full potential was emphasized repeatedly on the race circuits of the world and continued to reinforce the Jaguar legend.

**ABOVE**

*The United States provided Jaguar's major market for its long-lived range of XK sports cars, as typified here by this 1960 XK150 left-hand drive Roadster with its white-walled tyres, contrasting against the early aluminium-bodied XK120 Super Sports in the background.*

**LEFT**

*Jaguar's XK150 Coupé became a rare model within this legendary series, but is today one of the most renowned.*

# JAGUAR V-12
# E-TYPE

The E-Type Jaguar became a virtual totem for the 1960s, an emblem of the new prosperity hard-won by the Western world. Its supremely graceful and elegant original shape, masterminded by aerodynamicist Malcolm Sayer and Sir William Lyons, was nothing short of world-shattering when the original 3.8-litre 6-cylinder version was unveiled in March 1961. It offered genuine 140mph performance at a price so inexpensive it was little short of amazing. Jaguar had brought Supercar ownership within the reach of the only slightly above-average earner.

The 3.8-litre XK twin-cam engine gave 265bhp at 5,500rpm and the ton-and-a-quarter E-Type accelerated from 0-100mph in only 16 seconds. More significantly, one could cruise all day at 130mph and still have the scope to accelerate vividly in top gear!

In 1964, a new 4.2-litre version appeared, for the first time with synchromesh on bottom gear in a long overdue new manual gearbox. The new engine never felt as free-revving as the 3.8 it replaced. Both open two-seat roadster and coupé models were made plus the appalling 2-plus-2 Coupé with 9-inch longer wheelbase and ugly, more upright windscreen. The sports car 'feel' was being sieved out of the E-Type by such developments and new U.S. Federal Regulations

destroyed its looks from 1968 with front and rear light requirements, then choked-off its performance with emissions limitations. The E-Type was under sentence of death when in 1971 the ultimate variants emerged, launching Jaguar's eerily smooth yet exotic new 5.3-litre V12 engine. This two-cam unit never matched the charismatic sight and sound of a Ferrari but felt in every way more sophisticated. Even so, the E-Type's demise was in sight, and it came in 1973.

*Jaguar's E-Type series culminated in the 5.3-litre V12-engined 2+2 Coupé and Roadster models of the early 1970s. While the 12-cylinder engine proved wonderfully smooth and flexible, the E-Type chassis was showing its age, particularly the upright Coupé with all the U.S. Federal Regulation modifications necessary to light clusters at nose and tail. The Roadster carried them off more successfully.*

| JAGUAR V-12 E-TYPE 1973 |
| :--- |
| **Top speed:** 146 mph |
| **Engine:** 60-degree V12-cylinder |
| **Bore x Stroke:** 90mm x 70mm |
| **Capacity:** 5343cc |
| **Wheelbase:** 8ft 9ins (2667mm) |
| **Track:** 4ft 6½ins (front)/4ft 5ins (rear) - 1384mm/1346mm |

# JAGUAR XJ220

During the 1980s, Jaguar returned to the arena of World Championship motor racing by using the specialist Tom Walkinshaw Racing company as their proxy to tackle the contemporary Group C World Endurance Championship and, of course, the glittering promotional prize of Le Mans.

Using highly developed race-tuned versions of the production Jaguar V12 engine, TWR succeeded in their aim, winning the World title in 1987 and '88 and adding to Jaguar's 1950s tally of five Le Mans victories by winning the great 24-Hour classic in both 1988 and 1990.

Meanwhile, from 1987 the international collectors' car market had worked itself into a lather as record prices for old-established and very well-known cars were realized at auction, and the classic car trade followed where the specialist auctioneers set the pace. In 1987 the Ferrari F40 had been introduced, with

the Porsche 959 emerging almost in parallel and there seemed to be a 'silly money' market developing for such restricted production 'instant classics'.

This developing phenomenon was recognized by Jaguar and by TWR and a joint enterprise was launched to produce a Jaguar Supercar which eventually emerged as the XJ220.

The programme was unveiled at the Birmingham Show of 1988 and numerous eager and wealthy enthusiasts paid their £50,000 deposits to secure a place on the restricted order list. As events developed it would seem that most customers were money men first and enthusiasts second, if at all. They were mere investors eager to secure a car which seemed likely to be tradeable for a handsome profit once delivered.

However, Jaguar's preliminary presentation of their XJ220 was understood, at the very least, to include a V12 power unit which would have placed the car absolutely in the Ferrari, Lamborghini and ultimately McLaren F1 class. But by 1992 – 93 when the car finally emerged in the carbon-composite and metal it was powered instead by a 3.5-litre

version of the Rover V6 engine which had been developed from their light-alloy V8 essentially for the Metro 6R4 rally and rallycross car. This power unit, with induction boosted by twin turbochargers, lost its cachet as a collectable created by the original talk of V12 power and, although all customers had been made well aware of the change, Jaguar Sport – the company set up to handle the 220 – found itself confronted by a major problem.

During the XJ220's development cycle the international classic car market had collapsed. It hadn't simply faltered, nor moved wheezily into recession. It had deflated almost completely, with values reverting within a matter of weeks from totally unsustainable record levels to the kind of numbers which had been common in the early 1980s.

Against this background the XJ220 was not as attractive as it had once seemed to the money men, the investor customers, and a number simply reneged on their contracts to buy and kissed farewell to their deposit money. Jaguar Sport, however, refused to accept such

defections and commenced litigation against those who refused to honour their contracts. This seemed hardly the manner in which Jaguar would have behaved under Sir William Lyons' past control, for he would surely have sold such clients a fleet of saloon cars to the same value, thus retaining their good will for the future.

As it was, Jaguar Sport and the XJ220 became the brunt of enormous controversy and bitterness, and one heard of completed cars – unsold and unwanted – being consigned to long-term storage. Well into 1994, brand-new unregistered XJ220s seemed to be available for a fraction of their original list price.

One main problem cited was the unattractiveness of 'a cobbled-together Supercar powered by a *rallycross* Metro engine'. Another was the finished car's enormous size, some 6 feet wide, but with confined and claustrophobic cabin, poor headroom, and a forward view through the windscreen so shallow one felt as if one were peering through a pillbox gun embrasure. Seriously for a Supercar, the brakes also came in for some criticism.

Yet the car was undeniably fast, 210mph and 0-60mph in around 5secs. But the project had been tainted by the misfortune of its history and its timing. A sad story for what from many angles is essentially one of the most attractive of all modern Supercars, and a real tragedy for Jaguar and for its new owner, the Ford Motor Company. It merely goes to prove that there's more to a successful Supercar than superficial appearance.

**LEFT**
*Jaguar Sport's dark-blue No 1 production XJ220 of 1992 demonstrates the softly attractive, curvilinear styling which attracted so many to what should have been Jaguar's finest.*

**ABOVE**
*Adoption of the turbocharged Rover Metro 6R4 V6-cylinder engine for the XJ220 – in place of the more classical, naturally-aspirated Jaguar V12 – cost the project dear in terms of diminishing collector interest.*

---

### JAGUAR XJ220
#### 1992

**Top speed:** 220 mph

**Engine:** 90-degree 24-valve four-cam V6-cylinder twin turbocharged

**Bore x Stroke:** 94mm x 84mm

**Capacity:** 3498cc

**Wheelbase:** 8ft 8ins (2640mm)

**Track:** 5ft 7$\frac{1}{4}$ins (front)/5ft 2$\frac{1}{2}$ins (rear) - 1710mm/1588mm

# LAMBORGHINI DIABLO

Created by the Nuova Lamborghini company at their Sant'Agata HQ near Bologna, the Diablo was intended as the replacement for the renowned – in some quarters revered, in others reviled – Countach.

Ferruccio Lamborghini himself had long since sold out his interest to the French-based Mimran family, and in 1987 they had in turn sold out to the Chrysler Corporation of America which saw the Italian company as a passport to penetration of the highest class of automobile engineering and of the Supercar market.

Chrysler, in fact, even used Lamborghini to give them an entry into Formula 1, manufacturing purpose-built 3.5-litre naturally-aspirated V12 racing engines for supply to outside teams and, for one brief season, running Lamborghini F1 cars as an in-house factory team.

As a replacement for Countach, the Diablo emerged as a completely re-engineered device clothed in new coachwork re-detailed by Marcello Gandini which still, however, maintained the broad, low and long mid-engined Supercar shape adopted in such extrovert fashion in his extraordinary Countach.

Now the new Diablo was powered by a 5.7-litre V12 of similar specification to that of the preceding Countach S, and it was launched in January 1990.

While the original Diablo was a rear-wheel drive Supercar, in 1991 the four-wheel drive Diablo VT model emerged, the initials 'VT' standing for 'Viscous Traction' in homage to the proportional Ferguson Formula-device which divided torque transmission between front and rear wheels.

The Diablo's chassis frame was a basic welded steel tube structure, stiffened by add-on carbon fibre panels while the same ultra-light, ultra-rigid space-age material was also employed in some coachwork areas.

## LAMBORGHINI
## DIABLO
### 1994

**Top speed:** 201 mph

**Engine:** 60-degree four-valve four-cam V12-cylinder

**Bore x Stroke:** 87mm x 80mm

**Capacity:** 5707cc

**Wheelbase:** 8ft 8ins (2650mm)

**Track:** 5ft 0$\frac{1}{2}$ins (front)/5ft 4$\frac{1}{2}$ins (rear) - 1540mm/1640mm

In many ways the Diablo addressed and sought to correct some of the practical deficiencies of the Countach, and it certainly remained a remarkably rapid machine, the factory claiming a top speed potential of no less than 325km/h (201mph) and a 0-60mph acceleration time of around the 4sec mark. Certainly into the mid-1990s the Lamborghini Diablo continued to represent the most exotic of all the Italian motoring world's high-performance exotica.

**LEFT**

*Nuova Lamborghini's replacement for the widely-acclaimed but largely impracticable Countach has been the hardly less startling, rather more curvaceous, Diablo.*

**TOP LEFT**

*The Lamborghini Diablo's 5.7-litre four-cam, 48-valve V12 engine delivers a rumbustious 492bhp at 7,000rpm in standard form or 525bhp in the Diablo SE. While rear-wheel drive is normal, the Diablo VT variant provides a four-wheel drive option with 15 per cent torque-split to the front wheels.*

**TOP RIGHT**

*One of the Diablo's many striking features drawn from its Countach predecessor is the high-opening door geometry.*

# LAMBORGHINI COUNTACH LP 400S

Ferruccio Lamborghini was a highly successful tractor manufacturer and fast car enthusiast who, reputedly stung by a perceived slight from Ferrari over service of his highly expensive new car, swore he would have his revenge by building a rival Supercar of his own. And sure enough, by the end of the 1960s his Lamborghini cars, the front-engined P400 and the sensational mid-engined transverse V12 Miura, had made their name with speed, power and daring design and styling.

At the 1970 Turin Salon Lamborghini launched the mid-engined Urraco, a 2-plus-2 powered by a 2.5-litre engine, aimed plainly at the lucrative Porsche 911/Ferrari Dino market. That model's young designer, Paolo Stanzani, was then instructed to create a replacement for the Miura, Lamborghini's flagship model, which had become a legend in its own production lifetime.

Designer Stanzani worked closely on this Miura replacement with stylist Marcello Gandini of Carrozzeria Bertone, and their first prototype was unveiled as a show car to test public reaction at the Geneva Salon. Stanzani enlarged the familiar 4-cam V12 engine to 5-litres, placed it longitudinally in the rear behind the two-seat cabin but turned about-face so that its output end was down by the driver's hip. The gearbox was then mounted there to provide the most direct possible shift, avoiding the need for vague and lengthy gearchange linkages running back to the rear of the engine bay. Drive was then taken from the gearbox way back through the engine block to the final-drive at the rear. The new car's chassis frame was then to be shaped so that its outer surfaces would support the body panels direct, and meanwhile stylist Gandini's chosen form was outrageous, owing more to visual impact than practicality.

Lamborghini christened the finished car the LP 500, or *Longitudinal Posteriore Cinque Litri*. But Gandini's boss, Nuccio Bertone, evidently looked at Gandini's drawings and gasped *'Countach!'* – Torinese dialect for 'Cor!'

## LAMBORGHINI COUNTACH LP400S
### 1981

**Top speed:** 185 mph

**Engine:** 60-degree four-cam V12-cylinder

**Bore x Stroke:** 85mm x 73mm

**Capacity:** 4971cc

**Wheelbase:** 8ft 0$\frac{1}{2}$in (2450mm)

**Track:** 4ft 11ins (front)/4ft 11$\frac{1}{2}$ins (rear) - 1500mm/1520mm

– and Lamborghini simply adopted the exclamation as a perfect model name.

The result was typical of the Supercar world of the 1970s and '80s, in that the design had been driven in many ways by its outer envelope – its superficial appearance. Certainly the Countach looked as if it was doing 200mph when parked at the kerbside, but out on the road it was never as fast as it looked. Its interior heated-up rapidly in use, its seats were confined and uncomfortable, mere averagely tall drivers found their heads touched the rooflining unless they crooked their necks to one side, the windscreen pillar arched into the driver's forward vision, the side window rolled in against his temple, and the car was immensely wide. Its long doors threatened to strike a garage ceiling, and so the list went on. But no other manufacturer has ever produced a fundamentally more exciting-looking Supercar.

*Marcello Gandini's uncompromising body styling made the Lamborghini Countach LP400S the magnetic eye-catcher it proved to be, all vivid crease and joint lines, fins, wings and cooling louvres. This example is preserved in the Haynes Motor Museum at Sparkford, Somerset.*

# LOTUS ESPRIT TURBO

The original Lotus Esprit was a startlingly wedge-shaped, mid-engined exotic show car which had been styled by Giorgetto Giugiaro's young Ital-Design studio. But rather than being another mere expression of the 1970s' Italian 'folded-paper' school of styling, the Esprit had softer edges and rather more attractive – and less brassily 'glamorous' – lines than most.

Unfortunately, for a relatively small-engined Supercar, the Esprit added exceptional width to its remarkably confined height, which made it awkward to see out of and tricky to 'sight'. Its low build meant a deeply reclined driving position which in turn demanded a long door for adequate access, resulting in the already wide car needing even greater garage or parking space width to give the occupants any chance of opening the long doors wide enough to give

themselves a chance of escape.

But typical of a Lotus product, the Esprit also offered virtual track car reflexes and more lateral grip than almost any other production design.

In 1987, in-house styling changes made by the Lotus company at Hethel in Norfolk, England, further rounded-off and softened the edges of Giugiaro's, by that time, dating shape. But such work could not prevent the moulded glassfibre-bodied car feeling less crafted than assembled, 'as if from a plastic kit', as one former World Champion racing driver put it, which would always make it seem expensive in the market place.

Lotus's engine is a compact, light and powerful 2.2-litre 4-cylinder turbocharged unit, mounted amidships aft of the reclining-seated cabin, conferring more than adequate performance. And despite all criticism the car has also been most justifiably described as 'a Countach for a quarter of the price'.

---

**LOTUS ESPRIT
TURBO
1993**

**Top speed:** 161 mph

**Engine:** In-line 4-cylinder turbocharged

**Bore x Stroke:** 95.29mm x 76.2mm (2.2-litre)

**Capacity:** 2174cc

**Wheelbase:** 8ft 0ins (2440mm)

**Track:** 5ft $\frac{1}{4}$ins (front)/5ft 0$\frac{3}{4}$ins (rear) - 1530mm/1545mm

---

*The 1993 Lotus Esprit S4 shows off the softened lines which distinguished it from the earlier Giugiaro-styled Esprit line. Many observers considered that Lotus's mid-engined production coupé set new standards of handling and cornering power through the 1980s.*

# McLAREN F1

The British-based TAG-McLaren Group's Formula 1 racing team, McLaren International, became the most successful organization in Grand Prix history through the 1980s, its continual string of race victories and multiple World Championship titles with such drivers as Niki Lauda, Alain Prost and Ayrton Senna creating a glittering image of technical accomplishment and efficiency.

In 1988 McLaren cars won 15 of the season's 16 World Championship-qualifying GP races and only lost the last when their leading car, driven by Senna, was barged out of the race in the closing stages by a back-marker he was lapping at the time.

Design and operation of those 1988 McLaren cars was supervised by South African-born engineer Gordon Murray, who had become Formula 1 racing's most celebrated lateral thinker and design innovator in many years with the Brabham team.

Murray had long cherished the ambition of building what would

prove to be the ultimate driver's car – a Supercar for the road whose performance, practicality and behaviour would set a benchmark for the future unlikely ever to be matched, never mind exceeded.

TAG-McLaren's directors gave Murray the opportunity to build just such a Supercar in 1989 when a new subsidiary company named McLaren Cars Ltd. was set up across the road from the racing car plant in Woking, Surrey, south-west of London.

Murray ran the ensuing project as a benevolent dictator, establishing unshakeable targets and, at Monaco during the Grand Prix week in May 1992, the new McLaren F1 was unveiled to a startled and enraptured audience.

The car was a tiny mid-engined coupé, with three seats arranged in arrow-head formation inside the cabin, and with the forward central seat placing the driver absolutely on the centreline with Formula 1-style controls grouped around him.

Power was provided by the German BMW Motorsport Company of Munich in the form of a completely new and tailor-made, McLaren-only, 6.1-litre four-cam, fuel-injected V12

**BELOW**

*The McLaren F1's tailor-made 6.1-litre BMW Motorsport 'S70/2' V12 engine was a four-cam, 48-valver, an incredible 620bhp-plus unit entirely different from the Bavarian company's production 5-litre '850' V12. Instantaneous throttle response made the F1 the definitive, driver's car, a magical creation.*

**BELOW**

*Not so much a Supercar – more the World's first 'Ultracar'! Into the mid-1990s, Britain's amazing centre-drive McLaren F1 simply set matchless new standards for combined performance and practicality. It could transport three hefty 6-footers and bulky luggage in air-conditioned comfort at up to 230mph – and all in a package smaller than a 5-Series BMW saloon!*

engine delivering no fewer than 620bhp at 7,300rpm together with the most stupendous mid-range torque.

This simply outstandingly compact, yet powerful, V12 was incredibly efficient, burning unleaded fuel and meeting all contemporary international emissions standards. It drove through an ingenious 6-speed manual transaxle arranged with its final-drive output overlapping the clutch to minimize wheelbase length and so help minimize the McLaren F1 car's compact package size, and consequently its miserly overall weight.

The all-important power-to-weight ratio of the F1 was enhanced by its pure moulded carbon-composite full-monocoque construction, and emerged weighing little more than a mere 1,010kg – far less than the established Supercar norm. And although the likes of Lamborghini, Ferrari and Jaguar could only offer accommodation for two people and minimal baggage, the smaller McLaren F1 could swallow three hefty six-footers and their luggage which was

tailored to fit into twin helicopter-style lockers in each side, just ahead of the rear wheel arches. The car was supremely useable and practical.

Such Supercar superiority was reinforced by test driver Jonathan Palmer at the Nardo test track in Italy in 1993, when he clocked a top speed of 231mph in a prototype McLaren F1. For Gordon Murray this was a great step towards accomplishing his mission – even towards the invention of a new class. Forget the Supercar – McLaren had perfected the world's first Ultracar!

---

### McLAREN F1
#### 1993

**Top speed:** 231 mph

**Engine:** 60-degree 48-valve V12-cylinder

**Bore x Stroke:** 86mm x 87mm

**Capacity:** 6064cc

**Wheelbase:** 8ft 11ins (2718mm)

**Track:** 5ft 1$\frac{3}{4}$ins (front)/4ft 9$\frac{3}{4}$ins (rear) - 1568mm/1472mm

---

**BELOW**

*A crucial aspect of the brilliantly-packaged McLaren F1, the centre driving position with a passenger set back on each side contributed massively to the finest driver's car ever made, or ever likely to be made.*

**RIGHT**

*Typical of the McLaren F1's fine-grained design, its Peter Stephens-styled body incorporated a balance 'foil which opens under high-speed braking to prevent instability while also exposing extra air-intakes to cool the brake discs. The massive exhaust catalyser silencer doubles as a rear-end crushable structure for crash protection.*

# MASERATI GHIBLI

The Maserati company grew during the late 1920s and 1930s as a pure-bred racing car constructor, but after 1938 when it was taken over from the original five founding Maserati brothers by Modenese industrialist Adolfo Orsi, it branched out postwar into road car manufacture to capitalize upon the promotable success on track.

Orsi's Viale Ciro Menotti-based Maserati factory first entered the really high-performance production car market in the late 1950s when they launched the highly successful series of Maserati 3500 and 5000GT models.

What became the core of the company's subsequent *Gran Turismo* car production was then the big 4-cam Weber-carburettored V8 engine, a design master-minded by Chief Engineer Giulio Alfieri. This big belly-rumbling power unit had first been developed in 1956 – 57 for the 4.5-litre Tipo 450S sports-racing car which only narrowly failed to carry Maserati to the World Sports Car Championship title. The road-tuned version of this power unit then formed the heart of the marque's fine Quattroporte, Indy, Mexico and Ghibli GT cars and was also used mid-mounted in the Bora model.

The Ghibli was produced in both *Spyder* (open) and *Berlinetta* (close-coupled two-seat or 2-plus-2 seat) forms from 1966 to 1973 and *Berlinetta* production during that period totalled 1,149 units. Many regarded the Ghibli as Maserati's response to the Ferrari Daytona, and it was certainly a formidable competitor without ever achieving the same cachet as the Maranello product, examples of which still shone in competition at Le Mans, Sebring and Daytona; the Ghibli was never seriously developed for competition at any level.

But Maserati was always regarded by the *cognoscenti* as a company of considerably greater charm than Ferrari, and certainly the mind-set of its customer department staff often put

*The 1970 Maserati Ghibli Spyder had tremendous presence, a charisma not always reflected in its handling behaviour nor reliability. But it was undeniably fast – typical heir to Maserati's hard-won road racing reputation.*

## MASERATI GHIBLI
### 1970

**Top speed:** 154 mph

**Engine:** 90-degree V8-cylinder

**Bore x Stroke:** 94mm x 85mm

**Capacity:** 4719cc

**Wheelbase:** 8ft 4$\frac{1}{2}$ins (2501mm)

**Track:** 4ft 8$\frac{3}{4}$ins (front)/4ft 7$\frac{1}{2}$ins (rear) - 1440mm/1407mm

Ferrari's more aloof, even arrogant, attitude to shame. But Maserati also had a reputation for producing inadequately finished, poorly prepared cars whereas Ferrari could more confidently be expected 'to deliver the goods'.

Against this background, the 154mph Ghibli was actually more expensive in many world markets than the Daytona, perhaps because it was certainly a much rarer car, produced in smaller numbers. Its Carrozzeria Ghia styling had such an impact that it launched the career of Giorgetto Giugiaro as an independent designer, which alone made this bulky Maserati a landmark Supercar in more ways than one.

# MERCEDES BENZ 500SL

The Unterturkheim company's most modern, and most elegant, sporting SL – *Super Leicht* (Super Light) – series was launched at the Geneva Salon in 1989, comprising a common body/chassis powered alternatively by a range of in-line 6-cylinder, V8 or V12 engines.

The 6-cylinder option appeared in the 2.8-litre 280SL and 3.2-litre 320SL, the 5-litre V8 in the 500SL and ultimately the 6-litre V12 in the flagship 600SL.

Mercedes-Benz set out to establish new standards of sports car performance, safety, style and technology in these SLs with features including roll-over bar protection which automatically pops up should the car roll over, fully-automatic hood and aerodynamic hardtop and what was claimed to be the most advanced seat ever fitted in a production car.

This surprising feature incorporated a magnesium frame and integral seat belt, and an electronic memory system was provided which not only remembered the height,

backrest angle and headrest adjustment for different drivers, but also the position of the steering wheel and mirrors.

Automatically adjusting suspension was another feature, standard on the 600SL, with damping rates which would self-adapt as required to straight-line cruising or high-speed cornering, sharp braking and flat-out acceleration.

The four-valve per cylinder V8 engine of the 500SL featured four valves per cylinder like the most effective Formula 1 racing engines in competition, and had a quoted power output of no less than 308bhp, in comparison to the V12-engined 600SL's 389bhp.

The SLs were built upon a dedicated Mercedes-Benz production line not at Unterturkheim but at Bremen where each car was individually finished in a suitably high-tech factory which was unusual in featuring a highly polished and almost surgically clean wooden floor!

Overall, the SLs bristled with state-of-the-art technology; they were exquisitely well-finished, good-looking, sober yet suitably aggressive-looking, fast, capable and comfortable. Quite simply, they were splendid heirs to the revered three-pointed star emblem which has dominated the automotive engineering world for so many decades. Others aspire to Mercedes-Benz levels of product competence, but very few surpass them.

---

### MERCEDES-BENZ 500SL
#### 1989

**Top speed:** 155 mph

**Engine:** 90-Degree 32-valve V8-cylinder

**Bore x Stroke:** 96.5mm x 85mm

**Capacity:** 4973cc

**Wheelbase:** 8ft 3ins (2515mm)

**Track:** 5ft $0\frac{1}{4}$ins (front)/5ft 0ins (rear) - 1535mm/1525mm

# MERCEDES-BENZ 300SL

The giant German Daimler-Benz AG company's Mercedes-Benz line of production cars has always exemplified the highest technical standards. During the rare periods, only four of them, when Mercedes-Benz indulged in competition they did so with maximum investment of money, men and technological know-how and this uncompromisingly logical approach enabled them to dominate the Grand Prix world in 1908, 1914, 1934 – 39 and 1954 – 55. Having conquered all opposition on each occasion they would then retreat into their shell at Stuttgart-Unterturkheim, concentrating their magnificent design and engineering facilities upon producing excellence for customer sale.

Yet it must be appreciated that simple technical excellence of mechanical design and manufacture does not always equate with driving pleasure and realization of what enthusiasts would accept as 'a great car'.

For too many years, Mercedes-Benz remained wedded to a quirky rear suspension system which made their products tail-happy and rather unpleasant to drive at real pace. One of these was the legendary 300SL 'Gullwing' Coupé which was based upon a startlingly ingenious competition coupé design run by the factory team to win both the Le Mans 24-Hours and the Carrera PanAmericana road race in 1952.

**LEFT**
*The late Bob Roberts' 1955 High-Performance Mercedes-Benz 300SL Gullwing Coupé, shows off the high-silled, gullwing-doored lines of this revered but tricky to handle classic.*

**ABOVE**
*As counterpoise to the Gullwing Coupé, Mercedes-Benz catered for the 'Californian ragtop market' with the convertible Roadster 300SL like this 1957 example.*

The new 3-litre 6-cylinder engined coupé was based upon a multi-tubular 'spaceframe' chassis and clad in lightweight aluminium alloy coachwork. The high-level tubular truss members leading along each side of the cockpit area dictated the very high sill level in these areas, and to accommodate a practicable door opening size it became necessary to cut the opening panel in towards the centreline, through the car's roof section. In order to solve this problem, the Mercedes design staff decided to have two doors opening upwards in what has become the classical gullwing manner.

Where possible, the production 300SL which followed those 1952 works team racing prototypes used common mechanical parts with the 300 flagship saloon model, but the engine was uprated with dry-sump lubrication to prevent oil surge under high-G cornering loads and with Bosch fuel injection for optimum performance and throttle response. The engine ultimately delivered some 215bhp – rising in production to 240 – which endowed the Gullwing Coupé with tremendous performance by contemporary standards. But the cars retained swing-axle rear suspension, and the difference in rear-end adhesion between running with the

tail fuel tank full and empty was vivid.

Bought new in the mid 1950s and with U.K. taxes, the Gullwing cost £4,400 in Britain, which was as much as a Bentley R-Type luxury saloon. The model achieved almost instant cult status and surviving cars are today much sought-after and valuable collectors' items.

---

### MERCEDES-BENZ 300SL GULLWING
#### 1955

**Top speed:** 135 mph

**Engine:** 90-degree fuel-injected V8-cylinder

**Bore x Stroke:** 85mm x 88mm

**Capacity:** 2996cc

**Wheelbase:** 7ft 10ins (2388mm)

**Track:** 4ft 6$\frac{1}{2}$ins (front)/4ft 8$\frac{1}{2}$ins (rear) - 1384mm/1435mm

# MERCER RACEABOUT

The American Mercer Automobile Company took its name from the Mercer County of the State of New Jersey, U.S.A., in which it was formed. And among its range it was the Type 35 Raceabout which became its most famous model.

Chief Engineer Finlay R. Porter was responsible for the Raceabout's design and its initial version was introduced for public sale in 1911. Its specification was nothing very extraordinary, with power provided initially by an uncomplicated 4-cylinder Continental-built T-head engine which gave little more than 10bhp per litre at a somnolent 1,700rpm, driving through a three-speed gearbox. But while most contemporary cars of similar engine size and power would be encumbered with hefty coachbuilt bodywork, the Raceabout scored with its spartan body comprising nothing more than a bolster fuel tank at the rear behind two completely exposed bucket seats, with a boxlike forward bonnet concealing the engine and that distinctive monocle windscreen glass.

The crucial factor was that being so stark, the Raceabout weighed comparatively little and because of its lightness was able to pull a high-ratio back axle enabling it to cruise happily near its guaranteed maximum of some 70mph. Here was the Edwardian counterpart of the Caterham Seven!

By 1915 a more efficient 89bhp, 3,000rpm L-head engine had been adopted driving through a new four-speed gearbox, this Model 22 series design being the work of engineer E.H. Delling. But the new Raceabout's body had been extended to accommodate less austere public tastes. Why, it now featured such concessions to comfort as body sides and a bench-type front seat, and soon fully furnished touring models were also added to the company's range. Yet another new designer, A.C. Schultz, was made responsible for the Series 4 and 5 cars post 1919, and as their specification even included an electric self-starter, so the rakish, raffish old Speedster image grew ever more remote. These later cars could still top 75mph but Mercer meanwhile was on its last legs commercially and despite public interest in its wares plainly ebbing away. The company failed to change with the times and finally collapsed in 1925 not even surviving, as did so many of its great contemporaries, until the killing ground of the Great Depression at the turn of the 1930s.

### MERCER RACEABOUT
#### 1913

**Top speed:** 70 mph

**Engine:** In-line 4-cylinder

**Bore x Stroke:** 111.1mm x 127mm

**Capacity:** 4925cc

**Wheelbase:** 9ft 0ins (2743mm)

**Track:** 4ft 8ins (front)/4ft 8ins (rear) - 1473mm/1473mm

*The quintessential 'Cad's Car' of what to British enthusiasts is recalled as 'the Edwardian Period', the American Mercer Type 35 Raceabout, such as this 1913-built example, maximized performance by minimizing bodywork.*

# MORGAN PLUS-8

The Morgan Motor Company produces modern cars which are delightfully anachronistic in their obstinate refusal to depart from their traditional separate-fendered appearance rooted squarely in the 1930s. The Reverend H.F.S. Morgan began producing air-cooled engined three-wheelers at Malvern, Warwickshire, in the English Midlands, as early as 1910.

a tuned Standard Vanguard 70bhp engine in the Plus Four model and in 1954, with the 90bhp Triumph TR2 engine installed, the Plus Four became the first 100mph Morgan.

Into the mid-1960s the company briefly abandoned its traditional body style to dabble with a glassfibre-bodied streamlined coupé, the Morgan Four Plus Four, but it was discontinued after only 50 had been sold.

Then in 1968, when Triumph adopted 6-cylinder engines for its own products, Morgan required a new power unit, and they turned instead to

By 1927 the 'Moggy' Super Sports was good for 80mph completely standard but soon Morgan began to lose customers to the inexpensive new four-wheeled sports cars built, for example, by MG.

Consequently, in 1936, the first four-wheeled Morgan, the 4/4, was introduced, powered by an 1122cc Coventry Climax 4-cylinder engine developing 34bhp. The chassis remained light, the body spartan, and with the sliding-pillar independent front suspension which Morgan had always preferred, it steered and handled very well.

Postwar, in 1950, Morgan adopted

Rover for their lightweight, powerful and torquey GM-based 3½-litre V8. In the Morgan Plus Eight this 160bhp unit provided a top speed of 125mph, which many tuners and enthusiasts improved upon for competition.

In more recent times the Spring of 1988 saw a 2-litre 4-cylinder Rover-engined Moggie introduced, with 135mph good for over 120mph while the 185bhp Plus 8 in its latest form would achieve 130mph and accelerate from 0-60mph in a rumbustious 5.6 seconds.

Morgan have always catered to an acquired taste, and many faithful customers these days have the Moggie

for high days and holidays, and a conventional saloon for everyday use. The mere fact that the saloon might out-corner and out-handle the sports car is irrelevant, for despite its antiquated appearance the quality of the craftsman-built Moggy will be at least as good as the mass produced 'modern' sharing its garage.

### ABOVE

*Separate chassis, hand-assembled aluminium coachwork, separate fenders and external luggage racks and/or spare wheels are all features which were generally considered obsolescent in the early 1950s. 40 years on, the Morgan Motor Company keeps the faith.*

# PORSCHE 911 CARRERA 2.7 RS

The Porsche marque made its name during the 1950s with rapid development of air-cooled sporting cars of lightweight construction and aerodynamic form which were based upon Volkswagen components. The mainstream range of Porsche 356 Coupés and Spyders inspired a dedicated following and captured a large and lucrative market share throughout Europe, in the U.K. and the United States. The 356 remained in production for nearly 15 years but it became clear there had to be a replacement which would not be VW-based. Ferdinand 'Butzi' Porsche eventually headed the team which created that replacement, the Porsche 901 – introduced at the Frankfurt Show of 1963. However, Peugeot responded to announcement of the new model name by pointing out that they had reserved rights to three-digit car title serials with a middle zero, and so overnight the Porsche 901 became the Porsche 911, and a new legend had been born.

From its announcement in 1963, the Porsche 911 was powered by a 1991cc flat-six engine, until in 1969 an enlarged 2.2-litre variant was announced, offering improved torque and a maximum power output increased to a best of 180bhp from around 170. Two years later another hike was made, to 2.4-litres and 190bhp, and then in 1973 the largest engine option in the 911 range was further extended to 2.7-litres in a model which revived a popular and charismatic old title from Porsche racing history, the Carrera.

In the early 1950s there had been two classical open road racing events which fired public imagination more than any others. They were the 1,000-mile round-Italy Mille Miglia, and the amazing five-day Carrera PanAmericana run from border to border through Mexico. Porsche cars had excelled in the small classes in that exotic event and now the '2.7

Carrera' went on the market in limited numbers with its enlarged engine rapping out fully 210bhp in part thanks to its new Bosch K-Jetronic fuel-injection.

With greater mid-range torque, delivered lower in the rev range, the Carrera proved itself a tremendous performer on winding roads, and its 0-60mph acceleration time of under 6secs and maximum speed of 149mph combined with what had been developed into a well-balanced chassis to provide some hugely enjoyable high-performance motoring. I, myself covered many miles in a 2.7 Carrera and loved every moment of it – more than could be said for the larger, ultimately turbocharged models which replaced it. Certainly for many enthusiasts, Porsche reached a pinnacle of fine balance between power, torque, overall size, reasonably discrete appearance and chassis balance in the 2.7 Carrera which they never quite matched in any later product.

Today, well-preserved examples of this model are much sought-after and highly prized.

## PORSCHE 911 CARRERA 2.7 RS
### 1973

**Top speed:** 149 mph

**Engine:** Horizontally-opposed air-cooled 6-cylinder

**Bore x Stroke:** 90mm x 70.4mm

**Capacity:** 2687cc

**Wheelbase:** 7ft 5½ ins (2273mm)

**Track:** 4ft 6ins (front)/4ft 6ins (rear) - 1372mm/1368mm

*Revered by many Porsche enthusiasts as the finest of all 911s, the aluminium-panelled 2.7-litre Carrera RS lightweight of 1973 is very rare, and right-hand drive variants such as this are even rarer.*

# PORSCHE 959

In the late 1980s it became an act of faith for a major manufacturer to produce a limited-edition Supercar for sale to the super rich.

Porsche was no exception but its own tight-focused concentration upon technical excellence also, strangely, produced one of the least memorable Supercars of all. The Porsche 959 achieved all that one could reasonably expect but in such an unobtrusive and unexciting manner that it became one of the most strangely characterless

required to drive an F40 for another customer. The Ferrari 'fired up with an ear-splitting din. It had gaps around the doors you could see daylight through and was obviously thrown together, but in contrast to the beautifully executed Porsche the darned thing thrilled and frightened me to the core. I was ecstatic when I staggered away from it and will remember that first experience of the F40 for the rest of my life.'

Spot the difference? Here is plainly an example of Teutonic efficiency in sharp contrast to Italian flair!

The Porsche 959 was undoubtedly

PORSCHE 959
1988

**Top speed:** 195 mph

**Engine:** Horizontally-opposed air-cooled 6-cylinder twin turbocharged

**Bore x Stroke:** 95mm x 67mm

**Capacity:** 2851cc

**Wheelbase:** 7ft $5\frac{1}{2}$ins (2273mm)

**Track:** 4ft $11\frac{1}{4}$ins (front)/ 5ft 1in (rear) - 1505mm/1549mm

was no doubting the 959's speed potential, nor its tractive qualities.

When introduced it was the only production car capable of accelerating from 0-60mph in under 4seconds.

It may be that where Porsche are concerned one instinctively judges by standards one would not necessarily apply to the far cheaper Honda NSX, which by the same standards is competent and obedient though dull. But in a straight fight for charisma between Porsche 959 and Ferrari F40 the Italian appears to have the edge.

Supercars of all time.

This was exemplified for me by a friend who had the opportunity to collect a new 959 at Stuttgart, and drive it down to Geneva for delivery to a customer. Having parked the Porsche he walked away 'and simply forgot what I had driven down in'. He subsequently flew to Bologna and the Fiorano test track, where he was

as good as contemporary technology could make it. Porsche set about producing something supreme around 911-like dimensions, but with its computer-managed four-wheel drive system, six-speed gearbox, lightweight Kevlar/aluminium coachwork, air-cooled flat-six engine in the tail boosted by twin turbochargers to produce 450bhp at 6,500rpm, there

*The 1988 Porsche 959 was one of the earliest limited-edition top-value Supercars, its four-wheel drive sophistication truly stunning. This is the road equipped 'Comfortable Sports Version'. Features included tyre pressure monitoring, which might not matter at 70mph, but nearer 200mph the 959 driver would need to know.*

# PORSCHE 911 3.6 TURBO

Introduced for the 1993 model year, Porsche's latest version of the rear-engined turbocharged 911 line used the 6-cylinder opposed-piston air-cooled power unit already proven in the standard 911 Carrera 2 and Carrera 4. Torque had been improved to a massive 520Nm while also reducing specific fuel consumption.

Altered spring and damper settings and improved front brakes handled this boost in performance while the car rode on the fashionable modern 18-inch wheels which Porsche publicized as 'enhancing the classic look' of their be-spoilered 911 Turbo – but they alone cost well over £1,000 each!

By increasing the capacity of their brilliantly well-proven flat-six engine from the preceding 3.3-litre size to 3.6, peak horsepower was also increased from 320bhp to 360, sufficient to punch the Turbo's maximum speed over the 175mph mark while 0-60mph acceleration time was cut to less than 4.8 seconds!

But ever since its introduction, the idiosyncratic Porsche 911 had really been a triumph of development over design. Its engine was overhung outboard behind the rear axle to permit 2-plus-2 seating in the cabin space. This practical packaging move was anathema to most designers' view that concentration of mass within the wheelbase – between the front and rear axle lines – is a basic prerequisite for optimum cornering power and handling behaviour. The overhung engine mass promotes a pendulum motion when the car is cornered hard, and to control this characteristic endlessly juggled suspension geometries, tyre sizes and ultimately the duck-tail aerodynamic spoilers have been adopted. Ever more understeer – an inherent tendency for the front wheels to lose adhesion before the rears – was introduced and the cars became better balanced and tremendous fun to drive if one accepted the intolerably heavy pedals, their offset towards the centreline to avoid the front wheel arch bulge and the considerable tuck-in transition should one imprudently back off in corners.

But Porsche 911 Turbo-series performance has always been so awesome that, for most road drivers, there is self-evidently a whole area of performance which they are not inclined to explore. And for a self-proclaimed Supercar this is surely the most telling criticism?

## PORSCHE 911 3.6 TURBO
### 1993

**Top speed:** 175 mph

**Engine:** Horizontally-opposed air-cooled 6-cylinder twin turbocharged

**Bore x Stroke:** 100mm x 76.4mm

**Capacity:** 3600cc

**Wheelbase:** 7ft 4$\frac{1}{2}$ins (2270mm)

**Track:** 4ft 7$\frac{1}{4}$ins (front)/4ft 8$\frac{3}{4}$ins (rear) - 1405mm/1445mm

**ABOVE**

*Aerodynamic form has played a major role in Porsche styling ever since the marque's inception in 1946 with what became the range of 356 Coupé and Spyder models. Where their aerodynamic form maximized low power, the 3.6 Turbos help harness horsepower to spare.*

**LEFT**

*This 1993 Porsche 3.6 Turbo was top of their range costing £80,499 in the U.K. where this example's rather vivid colour scheme attracted considerable, but not always complimentary, comment!*

**RIGHT**

*Above all else the Porsche 911 variants such as the 3.6 Turbo have always been regarded as drivers' cars. Here the 2-plus-2 cockpit and controls of this flagship model offer rather more to the lover of style than to the older back-to-basics, performance-is-the-key, breed of Porsche fan.*

# SHELBY AMERICAN COBRA

The Anglo-American Cobra was the brainchild of Texan former Le Mans-winning racing driver Carroll Shelby. After heart trouble forced him to retire from driving in 1960, 'Ole Shel' sold his sports car dealership in Dallas and moved to southern California.

He was very shrewd and highly commercial, and his long experience of racing in Europe told him that while the handling manners of contemporary American muscle cars lagged behind European standards, the American V8 engine had enormous potential compared to complex and costly European equivalents.

The obvious compromise, he reasoned, would be to adapt inexpensive and reliable American V8 horsepower to a mainstream European sports car chassis. Those he chose were the 260 cubic inch (3.6-litre) 'Canadian X21' Ford V8 motor and the Ace chassis/body combination made by AC Cars of Thames Ditton, Surrey, in England.

The AC Ace was based upon a twin-tube 'ladder-frame' chassis with bodywork styled after the legendary Ferrari 166 *Barchetta* of the early 1950s. On February 16, 1962, Shelby's first AC chassis was flown to Los Angeles, where he had the lightweight V8 engine installed, together with an aluminium-cased four-speed manual gearbox. The combination scaled barely 100lbs more than AC's standard Ace with 2.6-litre 6-cylinder Ford engine, and it still retained 50/50 front/rear weight distribution.

It became the sensation of that year's New York Show. AC produced the body/chassis units in England, Ford Detroit the engines in America and Shelby American Inc. assembled the vehicles in Venice, California.

After only 75 of the 260 cubic-inch-engined cars had been built, the larger, much better, 289 cubic inch (4.7-litre)

Ford V8 was adopted for a further 584 Cobras – the bulk of production. Ultimately a monster variant emerged employing the big 427 and 428 cubic inch (7-litre-plus) Ford V8s, 348 being completed among which only 24 used the ultimate 428 option.

True to his background, Carroll Shelby encouraged private owners to race the cars and with Ford support ran his own works team, special Daytona Coupé versions actually humbling Ferrari to win the 1964 World GT Championship title.

The emergence of these Anglo-American cars upon the international racing scene set hearts a'beating for both competitors and spectators alike. The deep-chested rumble of the big V8s, especially the 427s/428s, provided a truly ground-shaking spectacle, accompanied by lurid wheel-spinning, tyre smoking power slides and lurches. There was little sophistication about these Anglo-American hybrids, but properly set-up they could be more forgiving than they looked, and incredibly fast! But they were also demanding to drive in contrast to more modern opposition, arguably requiring more muscle than brain. As Shelby himself said 'a belly-full of brave!'

---

## SHELBY AMERICAN COBRA
### 1966

**Top speed:** 140 mph

**Engine:** 90-degree V8-cylinder – in 4.2, 4.7 and 7-litre forms

**Bore x Stroke:** (289 cubic inch/4.7-litre) 00mm x 00mm

**Capacity:** 4727cc

**Wheelbase:** 7ft 6ins (2286mm)

**Track:** 4ft 7ins (front)/4ft 6ins (rear) - 1397mm/1371mm

**ABOVE**
*1965/8 Shelby American 7-litre Cobra. Ex-John Willment, with Ghia Body, this is one of the most exotic and lavishly equipped of all the Anglo-American cars.*

**RIGHT**
*1966 AC Cobra Mk III 289 – a lovely original example of the Cobra variant which many discerning enthusiasts regard as having been the best of the bunch.*

# SUNBEAM TIGER

Sunbeam had once been a majestic British marque. They were the only company active in genuine Grand Prix racing between the two World Wars and built not only World Land Speed Record-Breakers but also top-quality, high-performance road cars. The Depression years destroyed the company and the name became merely another string to the Rootes Group's bow, along with the undistinguished likes of Commer, Hillman, Humber and Singer.

Into the 1960s the Group was producing the pretty but really rather ordinary 1592cc Sunbeam Alpine sports, but the impact of the AC/Shelby American Cobra triggered untypical enterprise as a similar 4.2-litre American Ford V8 engine was squeezed into the Alpine chassis to produce the Sunbeam Tiger.

While the standard 4-cylinder Rootes engine had produced only 82bhp, the new V8 offered 141bhp at 4,400rpm, boosting top speed from a rather nervous 102mph to a comfortable 120, while 0-50mph plummeted from 9 to 7 seconds. The Tiger could be a handful on wet roads with wheelspin available at any toe-poke on the throttle, but it was relatively inexpensive and was well-received. The Rootes competitions department was very active, and they built highly-tuned, lightweight Tiger variants for both rallying and road racing. But when the American Chrysler Corporation swallowed the Rootes Group, there was plainly no future in their range for a hybrid sports powered by Ford! None of the Chrysler V8s were suitable and so after barely 8 months in production, the likeable Tiger was discontinued. It had been, in effect, a poor man's Cobra and was in many ways a better car than some may now recall.

**SUNBEAM TIGER**
**1964**

**Top speed:** 118 mph

**Engine:** 90-degree V8-cylinder

**Bore x Stroke:** 96.65mm x 73mm (Mk1) or 101.6mm x 73mm (Mk2)

**Capacity:** 4261cc (Mk1) 4737cc (Mk2)

**Wheelbase:** 7ft 2ins (2184mm)

**Track:** 4ft 1¾ins (front)/4ft 2ins (rear) - 1263mm/1270mm

*An Anglo-American hybrid, the 1964 Sunbeam Tiger successfully combined a body/chassis unit based upon the Rootes Group's handsome Alpine sports with an initial 4.2-litre (later 4.7) American Ford V8 engine. This is Don Pither's ex-works Rally version.*

# VAUXHALL 30/98

Long before Vauxhall became a mere satellite of the giant American General Motors Corporation, the name was a highly respected British marque which produced some of the most effective and best quality high-performance sporting cars of their day.

During the Edwardian motoring period before the First World War, sports-orientated motor manufacturers worked hard to publicize and promote their wares through competition success. Vauxhall Motors of Luton, England, dominated the fast, light, touring class with both factory and private-owner cars excelling in the sprint and hill-climb meetings which in those days dominated the British sporting scene. The 'Prince Henry' cars were enlarged to 4-litres in 1913 but even that model was threatened by the Talbots of the period, and so a prototype was built with a 4½-litre which was mounted into the light and nimble Prince Henry type chassis. The '30/98' denomination is said to have come from power output at 1,000rpm (30hp) against peak power at peak rpm – 98bhp.

Vauxhall guaranteed its chassis to attain 100mph in stripped competition form but before the First World War few 30/98s were sold; the Prince Henry being priced at £580 against a whopping £900 for the new model.

In 1919 the revival of the private car market permitted 30/98 production to resume as Vauxhall's top model. It became one of the most desirable of all sporting cars and was

## VAUXHALL 30/98
### 1924

**Top speed:** 80 mph

**Engine:** In-line 4-cylinder

**Bore x Stroke:** 98mm x 140mm

**Capacity:** 4224cc

**Wheelbase:** 9ft 9ins (2971mm)

**Track:** 4ft 6ins (front)/4ft 6ins (rear) - 1371mm/1371mm

*Every sober yet graceful line of the 1924 Vauxhall OE 30/98 emphasized the British marque's sophisticated high-quality engineering and standards of manufacture. While enthusiasts may sing Bentley's praises, true vintage car connoisseurs prefer Vauxhall's finest.*

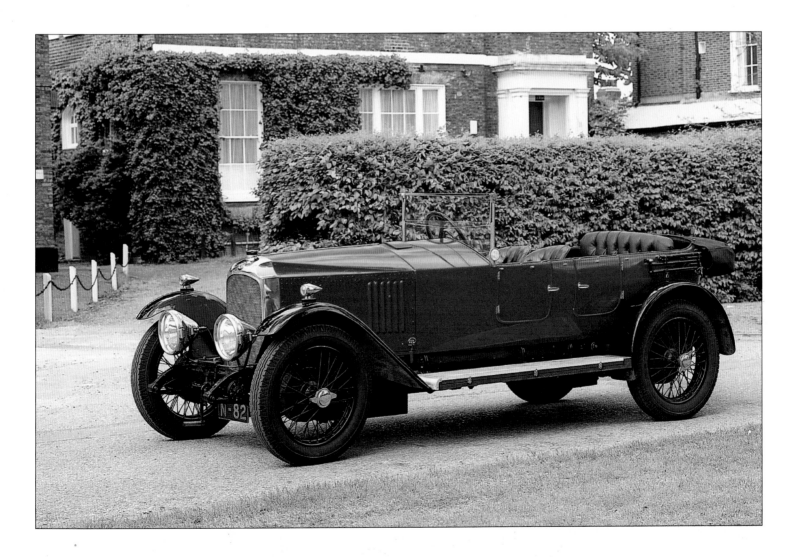

the fastest catalogued model from any British manufacturer.

On the road the E-Type 30/98 produced from 1913 – 1922 was a most exciting machine. Its power of 98bhp in a car weighing only 1.4 tons gave exceptional acceleration, 65 – 70mph and relaxed cruising at around that level. The 3:1 back axle ratio provided 31mph per 1,000rpm engine speed and, fully equipped, the cars would reach 85mph flat out. Yet all this in a comfortable, flexible and well equipped four-seater car. There is a story of a passenger prising himself painfully out of the rear seats of a 30/98 upon arrival at the Luton service department to be told 'We do think of them as two-seaters sir.'

Robust low-speed torque and a wonderfully sonorous exhaust beat balanced the mechanical noise of an engine notable for its wide valve clearance and straight bevel gears.

Pushrod overhead valve gear was then introduced on the OE 30/98 early in 1923, offering greater refinement than the side-valve E-Type. The OE engine offered enormous valves and ports. Less thunderous than the E-Type, it revved more freely to 3,300rpm and gave around 112-115bhp. It was also a quiet and durable engine. The 100mph chassis guarantee was maintained and 60mph in third gear and 80mph in top was standard performance fully equipped – stunning in an era in which large passenger cars would struggle to better 50mph. Performance of the OE never quite matched that of the E-Type but it was far more refined.

Third phase models subsequent to 1925 saw a new fully-balanced crankshaft, tandem drive for magneto and dynamo, conventional tappets instead of rollers and Autovac fuel feed. The balanced crankshaft and larger diameter bearings made the later OE 30/98 a beautifully smooth 4-cylinder – the ultimate in development freeing 120bhp at 3,500rpm.

After 1924 demand diminished, Vauxhall putting through occasional batches of 30/98s and by 1925-26 the Vauxhall appealed only to the more conservative buyer, unwilling to dabble in the new-fangled Bentley or Sunbeam. The chassis price of a $4\frac{1}{2}$-litre 30/98 was, however, only £25 more than that for a 3-litre Bentley.

A few Phase Four models were built featuring a redesigned gearbox and front wheel brakes where previously rear wheel brakes only and a transmission brake had been deemed sufficient. But the Vauxhall's new brakes were hydraulically operated and by 1927 this greatest of British vintage sporting cars was obsolescent and out of production.

*The engine of 1924 Vauxhall OE 30/98, chassis OE 101, demonstrates the architectural simplicity which was so typical of its times. Not that designer Pomeroy would not have incorporated all the electronic engine management multi-cam, multi-valve, variable timing technology of the modern Supercar – had it been available to him. But it was not.*